Never Beyond Hope

The extraordinary story of a drug mule who found Christ

Shepherd Pani with Jemimah Wright

Copyright © 2026 Jemimah Wright and Shepherd Pani

32 31 30 29 28 27 26   7 6 5 4 3 2 1

First published 2026 by Authentic Media Limited,
PO Box 6326, Bletchley, Milton Keynes, MK1 9GG.
authenticmedia.co.uk

The right of Jemimah Wright and Shepherd Pani to be identified as the Authors of this Work has been asserted in accordance with the
Copyright, Designs and Patents Act 1988.

All rights reserved.
No part of this publication may be reproduced, stored
in a retrieval system, or transmitted in any form or by any means,
electronic, mechanical, photocopying, recording or otherwise, without
the prior permission of the publisher or a licence permitting restricted
copying. In the UK such licences are issued by the Copyright Licensing
Agency, 5th Floor, Shackleton House, 4 Battle Bridge Lane, London SE1 2HX.

EU GPSR Authorised Representative
LOGOS EUROPE, 9 rue Nicolas Poussin, 17000, LA ROCHELLE, France
E-mail: contact@logoseurope.eu

British Library Cataloguing in Publication Data
A catalogue record for this book is available from the British Library.
ISBN: 978-1-78893-447-3
978-1-78893-448-0 (e-book)

Scripture quotations taken from
The Holy Bible, New International Version Anglicised
Copyright © 1979, 1984, 2011 Biblica
Used by permission of Hodder & Stoughton Ltd, an Hachette UK company.
All rights reserved. 'NIV' is a registered trademark of Biblica UK
trademark number 1448790.

Scripture quotations marked 'KJV' are from The Authorized (King James) Version.
Rights in the Authorized Version in the United Kingdom are vested in the Crown.
Reproduced by permission of the Crown's patentee, Cambridge University Press.

Scripture quotations labelled 'The Passion translation' are from The Passion
Translation®. Copyright © 2017, 2018, 2020 by Passion & Fire Ministries, Inc.
Used by permission. All rights reserved. ThePassionTranslation.com.

Cover design by Jennifer Burrell at Fresh Vision Design
Printed and bound by CPI Group (UK) Ltd, Croydon, CR0 4YY

Some names have been changed to protect privacy of individuals

To the Author of Life, my Lord and Saviour, Jesus Christ – for his grace, guidance and unending faithfulness.

To my beloved wife, Zuzeka – thank you for your unwavering love, support and encouragement through every season.

To my children – Zizo, Zintle, Nkazimulo and Nqobile – may this be a testament that with God, all things are possible. Never stop believing.

To the Coffman family – thank you for allowing God to use you so that his purpose and will could be fulfilled in my life. I thank you, and I thank God for placing you in my path for this assignment.

One of the great privileges of my life is travelling the world and meeting people like Shepherd, who through the power of the gospel have gone from being the problem, to providing a solution. This really is a great Jesus-only story. Read on and be inspired.

Andy Hawthorne, OBE, author, founder of The Message Trust

What an encouraging and inspiring read! There is no life beyond hope. God is on the move in prisons in South Africa and beyond! Thank you Shepherd for sharing your story.

Simon Guillebaud, author of Choose Life: 365 readings for radical disciples

The life story of Shepherd Pani is more than just a book – it's a powerful window into a life that began with deep struggles, shaped by painful roots, and was radically transformed by a divine intervention. God's grace not only changed his direction but set him on a completely new path, free from the weight of his past.

As 1 Peter 1:18 says, 'For you know that God paid a ransom to save you from the empty life you inherited from your ancestors.'

I found it hard to put this book down. It was inspiring, motivating and deeply encouraging to witness a life, once headed for destruction, rescued by the loving pursuit of a Heavenly Father. I'm proud to have played even a small role in Shepherd's journey and the man he has become. A truly remarkable book – well written, deeply moving and an easy, impactful read.

Pastor Andre Roodt, founder of Luthemba Lethu Community Project

Shepherd's story is not only one of gospel triumph, and of change both moral and religious, but also an in-depth first-person look at life in the poorest sections of Cape Town, and of South Africa. This autobiography of moral transformation highlights the importance of Christian ministries and services in prison, with ex-offenders, in job creation, in start-up funding, and crucially in the role of Bible-teaching churches. It seems the whole range of Christian help was garnered together to bring Shepherd from darkness to light, from the past and into his future.

Lex Loizides, pastor of Jubilee Community Church

We first met Shepherd Pani at one of our monthly prayer days in 2017. He immediately impressed us as someone who faithfully wanted to follow God. Over the following months and years, it has been a joy to get to know him better and celebrate all that God has done in and through him. Shepherd was determined not to let his past – whether his lack of opportunities, personal challenges or mistakes – define his future. He was hungry for God and eager to learn.

This quiet resolve has shaped him into the man he is today: a devoted family man, committed to Jesus and to continued growth. We are so glad his story is now being told in this book. It will inspire many and stands as a powerful testimony to God's grace and goodness.

Tim and Christina Tucker, The Message Trust

In life, many stories remain unwritten; this is one I'm deeply grateful has made it to print. Shepherd's story is a powerful reminder that no life is beyond the redemptive power of God.

I've known Shepherd for close to ten years. I first met him during my time at The Message Trust when he joined our reintegration programme. Immediately, I recognized a young man passionate about Jesus and determined to make good choices and build a better future.

Over the years, I've watched Shepherd grow into a devoted husband, a loving father and someone who loves God and his family deeply. He has become a close friend, and I am so thankful for the incredible transformation God has brought about in his life, now using him to impact many others walking similar roads.

This book is a testimony of a man who made some of the worst decisions, yet through grace, learned to make the right ones, even in the hardest of seasons. As Shepherd's life so clearly reflects, 'What the devil meant for harm, God turned around for good.' May this story inspire you and bring hope to those in spiritual darkness, that they too might find the light that comes from knowing Jesus, just as Shepherd did.

Mark Slessenger, Advancement Manager at Living Hope, former deputy CEO of The Message Trust South Africa

This is not just another compelling life story – far more even than a riveting account that inspires. The book you are holding will stir your spirit, expand your perspective and awaken a deeper hunger for something more, providing a deeply personal insider view of the stark realities of life in South Africa and the challenges and triumphs millions live through every day. From the dusty streets of Cape Town's townships to the seductive lure of Brazil's high-end drug scene, my friend Shepherd's journey is raw, real and redemptive. It will transport you into a world few have lived to tell about – and leave you with a burning desire to forsake the trivial and live fully for the Kingdom.

Mkhululi (MK) Letsatsi, Executive Director of
United in Crisis South Africa

Contents

Foreword		*xi*
1	The Worst and Best Decision of My Life	1
2	Going to the Eastern Cape	6
3	No Education	17
4	Losing My Father	22
5	'You Want to Smoke?'	27
6	'X the Unstoppable'	36
7	Cheese Boys	44
8	Life Unravelling	52
9	Getting a Job	59
10	Near Death	66
11	Brazil, 2011	77
12	'Why is My Life Like This?'	87
13	'If You Help Me Get Back to South Africa, I Won't Do This Again'	95
14	My New Home	107

15	My First Bible	117
16	Being Discipled	130
17	F-section	142
18	Healing Old Wounds	151
19	'Are You Ready to Go Outside?'	162
20	Divine Appointments	171
21	The Future and Coffee	177

Epilogue – 2025   *189*

Foreword

If you were to meet Shepherd for the first time, you would have a hard time believing he once sat down in a Brazilian favela for a dinner of cocaine pellets. Maybe only his miscellaneous tattoos would betray him.

Can a person render their life unredeemable? Can you fracture your life to such an extent that it's irreparable? Can you go too far? Pass the point of no return?

Shepherd felt this way. I felt this way. I guess that's why we connected. We had common ground. He found God behind bars in a Johannesburg prison, I met God while I was running from a bad trip on magic mushrooms. Shepherd had been walking this journey for a number of years, I had two weeks under my belt. We met at a monthly prayer meeting in 2017 when I was interning with the Message Trust. I providentially grabbed a seat next to him and we struck up a conversation. We only spoke for a few minutes. But – this I remember – it was electric. It was the first time, apart from with my parents, I was discussing the new life I had been experiencing. I found out, I wasn't alone in my discovery. We both had felt the living waters of God flow through our veins. And we wanted more of it. I had found a fellow seeker. A kindred spirit. I didn't want our conversation to end. I spent the rest of the day skipping around Cape Town like a caffeinated springbok.

On my first trip back to South Africa in October 2018, I introduced Shepherd to my mom. Over dinner, I asked him to share his story with her. By the end of it, the table next to us had stopped talking, they were leaning ever so slightly, unashamedly pointing their ears in our direction. I trust you'll have the same response. Even though most of us haven't swallowed any cocaine pellets, nor faced charges of ten years in a South African prison, I hope you'll see yourself in Shepherd's story, and find what he did.

> For to him that is joined to all the living there is hope: for a living dog is better than a dead lion.
> *Ecclesiastes 9:4, KJV*

Jeremiah Coffman
Los Angeles, USA

1

The Worst and Best Decision of My Life

I was directed into the kitchen, in the boss's apartment. The windows were open and it was already dark outside. Sweat was trickling down my back. It was hot in Brazil, but I was also nervous.

'Sit here, X,' my friend, Emmanuel, said as he pulled out a chair at the dining-table.

Laid out on a cloth on the table in front of me were line after line of two-and-a-half-inch bullets of cocaine. They looked like fat, bloated mealie worms encased in thin plastic wrapping. I was going to have to swallow each one, and carry them in my stomach back to South Africa. I gulped hard when I saw them, my mouth suddenly dry. As if knowing my need, Emmanuel placed a two-litre bottle of cold Pepsi from the fridge on the table.

'You'll want this,' he said with a smile.

I smiled back, feigning confidence, and poured myself a glass, taking a sip and washing the cool liquid around my mouth.

I knew I could do it, as I'd done it before, but it wasn't going to be easy.

When I had first seen the cocaine bullets on my previous trip I was shocked at the size. 'This won't go down,' I said.

'Oh, they will,' Emmanuel had laughed. 'If you need something to go down your throat bad enough, you can get it down.'

I remembered his words and took a deep breath; *how had I got myself into this situation?*

I knew the sooner I started, the sooner I could get on my way, and begin the rest of my life. I picked up the first bullet, placed it in my mouth, tilted my head back and had a drink of Pepsi. It got halfway down my throat, and then stopped. Quickly I took another swig of Pepsi before the gag reflex bought it back again. I swallowed and drank another mouthful, it went down, but I felt it all the way. It was very uncomfortable, and this was just my first bullet. Emmanuel was sitting on a plastic chair next to the open door of a balcony looking at his phone. He knew this would take a long time, so was settling in for the long haul.

Slowly but surely I worked my way through the pile. At one point, after swallowing a few bullets, I took a drink and walked out to the balcony for some fresh air, letting the cocaine go down into my stomach. I could see lights twinkling from the neighbourhood houses on the hill above us, and some below as well; it was pretty. I listened to the sounds of a community going to sleep, doors shutting, dogs barking, but sleep was a long way away for me.

'OK?' asked Emmanuel, after a few minutes.

I snapped back into the moment and to the job in hand.

'Yebo,' I said, returning to the table.

A few times in the process I did gag, and had to have a pause, to gather myself before starting again. At some points I got into a bit of a rhythm as I methodically slid each bullet down my throat with a swell of Pepsi. I knew it was mind over matter, so I just told myself I could do it, it was no problem. The whole process took about two-and-a-half hours. I had a few toilet breaks to pee and, when the last bullet went down, I felt I understood what it was like to be pregnant. My stomach was so full. I prayed the cocaine would stay in until I landed in Johannesburg.

'Nice, X,' Emmanuel said, standing up and stretching as I finished. 'You are a natural.'

I smiled, one hand stroking my bloated belly. I was a skinny guy, and with my shaved head looked younger than my 22 years. Hopefully my innocent-looking face would work in my favour when I went through customs.

I knew I was a walking target once all the cocaine was inside me. We had heard stories of Nigerian gangs kidnapping mules, ripping open their stomachs, removing the goods and leaving the person for dead. I also knew that if one burst inside me for any reason, I would die immediately. It was a massive risk, and I planned that this would be my last time.

It was now after midnight; I had a few hours to lie down on the sofa before going to the airport in São Paulo. At 3 a.m. Emmanuel came to wake me up.

'OK, let's get you to your flight,' he said. I opened my eyes and nodded. Getting up cautiously, I went to collect my bag.

I didn't say much on the drive, I just looked out of the window at the Brazilian countryside. They dropped me at the airport with brief words of good luck, and then I was alone.

I was flying Emirates via Doha to Johannesburg. Not direct this time. Maybe they got me that ticket to try and hide that I was coming from Brazil – a known country for drug smuggling. I knew I must not eat oily food or drink alcohol to calm any nerves. So stone-cold sober, filled with cocaine, I boarded the plane.

From São Paulo to Doha I felt so tired, and my stomach was uncomfortable. When we landed in Doha airport, I knew I had to go to the toilet. I quickly made my way to the nearest bathroom and, as I sat down on the seat, I had to go. I winced as I realized bullets were coming out.

I cursed, and looked into the toilet bowl – there were four cocaine capsules floating in the water. There was a lot of money in each bullet; however, I had no choice but to flush them away. If I was caught with them, I would go straight to prison in Doha, and I dreaded to think how long for.

Feeling frustrated, I went to the gate for my final flight to Johannesburg. It was about six hours. I tried to get comfortable in my economy seat. At least I was by the window and I could distract myself by looking at the clouds and land far below. In the end I just closed my eyes and attempted to sleep. There was an older foreign lady sitting next to me; she didn't speak English, so we just smiled politely at each other.

As the flight was beginning its descent into Johannesburg, I realized I needed the toilet again. I had only eaten a roll, some water and orange juice on the flight, but my stomach was feeling terrible.

I gently put my hand on the arm of the lady to get her attention, motioning that I wanted to get up and needed to get past her. As she slowly pushed herself out of the chair, I unbuckled my seatbelt, squeezed past, and walked cautiously to the toilet at the back of the plane, trying not to catch the eye of any of the air stewards, in case they told me to sit back down. I was sweating as I closed and locked the door of the tiny cubicle. As I sat on the toilet bowl, my stomach contracted, and again

I felt bullets come out. This time there were six. My heart sank, but I had to think fast. I whisked them out of the toilet, washed them down carefully, and placed them in tissue in my coat. I stayed in the toilet for a while, debating what to do. If I flushed them, it would mean I wouldn't get paid my full fee, which was already reduced from the four I had lost in Doha. I took a deep breath and decided to risk it. Cautiously, I made my way back to my seat, and gave the old woman a faint smile in thanks as she stood up for me to sit down.

As soon as we landed I sent an SMS to my friend, Rasta. 'Six have come out, should I flush them?'

Immediately I got a response. 'No! Don't flush them. I'll send someone to get them.'

I had no idea how he would do that, but I trusted him. I knew they always had people watching us. I believed, now I was back in my homeland, he had contacts who would help me. I placed the cocaine bullets carefully into the small pack I wore over my chest, and prepared to disembark.

It was both the worst and best decision of my life.

2

Going to the Eastern Cape

When I was 6 years old, my father, who I called Tata, decided it was time to show me where my ancestors were from. He planned to take me on the long journey back to his birthplace in the Eastern Cape of South Africa, just outside a town named Butterworth.

Before we travelled, he told me we needed to get protection for the journey from a sangoma. Sangomas are African traditional healers, who are seen as being a channel for ancestral spirits, making contact and communicating with the ancestors on behalf of the people. Tata wanted our ancestors' protection on the 700-mile drive back to the Eastern Cape. So the next Saturday early in the morning we set out to visit the sangoma in Nyanga township (Nyanga is Xhosa for 'moon').

'Tata, what will the sangoma do?' I asked my father as we drove in his old, red Toyota Corolla.

'He will give offerings to our ancestors for safety on the journey. You are my first-born from your mother, I don't want anyone to put a curse on you.'

I looked at him with wide eyes from the front passenger seat.

My father used to wear two straps on his upper arms, inside each was muti (medicine) from the sangoma. It was also supposed to protect him from harm. I never asked about the muti, although I wasn't told not to, I somehow knew that it was secret. In Xhosa culture no one talks about the charms and protections from the sangoma.

The sangoma we were going to see in Nyanga was very well known, and expensive. He was frequented by the prosperous men and women – the taxi-cab owners and others like them.

We arrived in Nyanga, a community of corrugated-iron shacks and small government-built houses. It was hot, being December, and busy, with people shouting out to each other, and cars driving by. Tata stopped close to the Golden Arrow bus terminus. After he had parked his car, we walked the short distance to the sangoma's house. I wanted to take my father's hand, to get some reassurance, but I did not reach out.

Even though I was a little anxious, I trusted my father, and believed he would protect me from anything that was bad. There was a small line of people waiting to see the sangoma in the front room of his house. There were two benches against the wall, with people sitting as in a doctor's waiting-room, but this was for a witch doctor. My father and I sat down, my legs dangling, not yet able to reach the ground. A man in his twenties worked for the sangoma, and he directed people out when it was their turn. My legs were feeling sweaty on the seat because it was such a hot day, but eventually the man motioned to my father, who nodded to me. It was our turn.

We walked through the house towards a pungent smell of burning herbs and incense out back. Once out of the house there were lots of different plants growing, and a small shack in front of us; this was the sangoma's treatment room. My father went in first; the door was very small so you had to crouch down to enter. He spoke to the sangoma, and then called me in. I knelt down and crawled into the dark, smoky space, blinking as my eyes got used to the dim light. There were no windows, so the only light came through cracks in the walls and through the doorway. I gasped when I saw a huge dead baboon hanging from the roof. Its flesh and main bones had been removed, so it was just the skin; however, the bones of the hands and head were intact. I could smell burning herbs coming from somewhere and it made my head dizzy.

My father placed our cash payment in a bowl, and then the sangoma beckoned me forward. I watched the man shyly; he did not speak a word to me.

I noticed a dead mountain lizard on the ground. The witch doctor cut bits off the reptile to make the muti. He motioned me to take my shirt off and give my arm to him. I looked at my father, and he nodded. The witch doctor made some cuts on my wrist with a razor blade and then at every other joint in my body. He then mixed a black paste with skin from the dead lizard and rubbed it into every cut.

I flinched and held my breath. The paste stung my flesh and the smell was horrible. The whole ceremony took about twenty minutes, and soon we were out in the fresh air again. I was relieved both that it was over, and that I was now protected from any curses. If my father believed in it, then I did too.

To celebrate, my father went to buy some meat to *braai* (barbecue) close by, and that evening he cooked it for our family supper.

My father was 31 and my mother 32 when I was born and I was their first child together, although Mama had a boy and two girls from a previous relationship; Lungile, Pamela and Phumeza. My father also had a child from a previous relationship, a son, Khumbulani. I didn't meet this half-brother, the spitting image of my father, until he came to introduce his wife to us when I was about 12.

Mama lived with her three children and mother, Cinci, in Gugulethu township, a community of shacks and pot-holed streets. It was a place of noise and life, as well as desperation and poverty.

In 1976, when my father, Mongezi Pani, was 18, he travelled from the Eastern Cape to join his older brother, Mncoseleli, who was working for a family who lived in Camps Bay, a beautiful and affluent suburb of Cape Town.

My mother was working in the kitchen at Spur, the fast-food restaurant, in the Golden Acre shopping centre in the central business district (CBD) of Cape Town, when she met my father in 1987. They were both on a lunch break and ended up eating together. They became a couple soon after, although they only married in 1995, after I was born. In 1993 my younger brother, Christopher Vukile, was born. When my parents got together, they moved to a shack in Phola Park, Gugulethu, next to Cinci, who lived with Mama's older three. I spent the first six years of life there. Tata heard that the city refuse department needed drivers, and the salary was much higher than he was getting as a refuse collector. In the evenings he would come home and take driving lessons in Khayelitsha until he had passed his test. He then got a job as a driver.

I always thought of Lungile, Pamela and Phumeza as my full brother and sisters, as my father treated them as his own. Tata taught Lungile to drive, and later took him to the Eastern Cape to become a man, a rite of passage in the Xhosa culture.

My parents, myself and Vukile eventually moved to a small, two-bedroom, concrete bungalow on 19 Hobohobo Street in Litha Park, an area of Khayelitsha township. It had wooden shutters on the windows, a tile roof and burglar bars. There was a metre-high, steel fence all the way around the property, and my father added a double garage in later years. It was small and simple, but it was home.

In the year we moved to Hobohobo Street, Cinci was given land in the new township community of Samora Machel on the Cape flats. She built a small house on the land, and my older two siblings lived with her. My older sister, Phumeza, stayed with us and went to Lwandla Primary School in Khayelitsha. She shared a bed with Vukile and me until she eventually moved to go to a coloured high school closer to Samora, where they taught in English.

To give a bit of background, South Africa is known as the rainbow nation after Archbishop Desmond Tutu used the phrase to symbolize our nation's diverse cultures and ethnicities coming together in unity after years of racial division. About 81.7 per cent of South Africa's 63 million people are black, 8.5 per cent coloured, 7.2 per cent white and 2.6 per cent Indian/Asian. In South Africa, 'coloured' refers to people of mixed European, African and Asian ancestry, and is a distinct racial group in my country. I grew up around mostly black people in Khayelitsha.

Samora, where Cinci lived, was also mostly populated by black Africans. Cinci spent hours cultivating her garden; she had tomatoes, potatoes and other vegetables, as well as flowers that she would prune and tend. Her house was always clean and tidy, and her garden well looked after. My grandmother was a Christian woman, and I am sure she prayed for me. She didn't drink or smoke, and she walked with elegance and authority, but I remember thinking she was difficult when I was young as she was so strict. We had to work if we stayed at her house during the holidays, and she kept a short cane on her at all times, to hit us if we were out of line.

Once I was playing in the field with friends in the holidays. I came home after her 6 p.m. curfew. I walked into the house, and realized as soon as I saw her face that I was in trouble.

'My boy, do you know the time?' she asked, not waiting for an answer. 'I sleep early and I don't allow you to come in late. This is not Litha Park, I am not your parents. You must obey my rules.' She walked towards me and thwacked her stick on the back of my legs.

I yelped and tried to get out of her way. 'Sorry, Cinci, sorry,' I pleaded.

'OK, go to your room,' she said, and that was the end of it.

Cinci would read her Bible at 6 p.m., go to sleep at 7 p.m., and then was up at 5 a.m. In the morning before dawn, she drank hot tea on the porch outside. She made both tea and coffee in bags that she boiled on the stove, so that they were very strong. Cinci started work at 6 a.m., so I also had to get up then if I was visiting. She would say, 'OK, my boy, you have come to visit, you need to wake early.' I hated it because I wanted to sleep.

Even though she was stern I respected her. Cinci spoke many languages: Xhosa, Afrikaans, English, Sotho, and Fanagalo, an African pidgin language that was developed during the colonial period to promote ease of communication in South Africa. Mama and Tata did not discipline me as Cinci did; maybe it was Mama's reaction to her childhood, she wanted to raise her children differently. I think my mother's attitude to discipline had been a pendulum swing in the opposite direction, as Vukile and I were allowed to run free with very few consequences. My older siblings had a different childhood, as they stayed with Cinci.

I remember my early childhood being happy. During the week, Litha Park was quiet as everyone was at work but, at the weekend, the streets were alive with people, women doing their washing and hanging it along fences to dry, children playing, and men gathering to sit and talk outside their homes.

I would spend my days playing either soccer or cricket with my friends: Umvuso, Siya and Lucky. Lucky lived a few doors down from us; he was older than me and very smart, I admired him like a big brother. His family sometimes invited me to go with them to the Catholic church. I disliked the strong smell of incense in the sanctuary, but I loved being with Lucky. His family also mixed their churchgoing with ancestor worship, like Cinci and many other Xhosa and Zulu families.

My mother went to the Universal Church in Mitchells Plain. I remember one Sunday going with her. Vukile and I were placed in the children's church and, as I was a curious boy, I decided to explore the building. I went into one room and on a table saw a huge mason jar with a white lid. Inside were what looked like tiny rats in jelly. I was terrified, and ran out of that room as fast as I could. I told Mama later that I would never go back, and that was the last time I stepped into church for a long time.

Tata never went to church, he believed fully in ancestor worship. The day after my trip to the sangoma when I was 6, we left by bus to go to Butterworth. Mama stayed at home with Vukile.

It would be the first time I met my father's mother. I called my grandmother 'Makulu', translated it means 'the mother that is old'. It is a term of respect. She was a slender lady with short grey hair. She wore traditional clothing in bright coloured fabrics, a long skirt with a blouse, and always a simple scarf around her head.

Makulu lived in a one-room, mud-brick rondavel house with a thatched roof, a door and window. She owned two more rondavels – a cook house and a third rondavel in the middle where my dad slept. There was another hut with a long-drop toilet, but I was scared I would fall down the deep, dark, stinking hole, so I always ran into the field to do my business. My grandmother knew what I was doing, and didn't seem to mind. I think she was also scared I would fall down the long drop!

I felt my grandmother's love; she would take me around the village, introducing me proudly to the other *gogos* (grandmothers) as 'the son of her son'. I slept on a mattress on the floor in her rondavel with Mimi, my cousin, the son of my father's brother. Mimi was born before my uncle met and married his wife, so Mimi stayed in Butterworth, looked after by our grandmother. His father had died in 1985 in a car accident in Swellendam on the way back to the Eastern Cape, so Mimi was now fatherless. He was about ten years older than me. In those days it was believed children should grow up in the father's home, which is why he was with Makulu, and not his own mother.

Before bed each night Makulu would tell us detailed and wonderful stories. There was one about a wolf that would come into a village at night to eat the sheep. Two guys in the village saw the wolf and hid from it in a big pot. I loved her stories, and I would fall asleep happily after they ended.

The village had no electricity or running water. Water was collected either from the river in buckets, or from rain water that poured into containers kept by each rondavel. It was then boiled over the fire, and used for drinking. If it rained the ground became very muddy and it rained a lot in the summer months.

After a few days in the village, when I thought Tata had just gone to the shops, he travelled back to Cape Town without me. I had not realized that my father was going to leave me there for three weeks of the December holidays. I remember crying, wondering what had happened to him.

For the first few days the villagers told me that my mother was coming to get me by bus. The bus stop was in another village so, each day, with a group of children I walked there and sat at the stop, waiting. In the Eastern Cape there was very little traffic, so it was only about every three hours that a car would come through. I would see a vehicle in the distance, shimmering like a mirage in the heat, and stand up hopefully, shielding my eyes from the sun to get a better view. I held my breath, praying for the car to slow down, stop, and for my mother to get out, but it never happened.

One day, I was walking to the bus stop alone and it started to rain, but it wasn't normal rain, it was hailing, and the hailstones were bigger than anything I had ever seen. Initially, being a young city boy, I thought I was being hit by golf balls. I couldn't understand what was happening. I ran to find shelter when a lady grabbed me and pulled me into her rondavel, protecting me from injury. I peered out of the window, and witnessed the death of a chicken as a hailstone hit it head on. I didn't carry on to the bus stop that day.

Eventually I realized everyone was lying to me, and my mother wasn't coming. I don't think they were being mean to me, there was just not much to do in the village, and the long walk to the bus stop would be a distraction.

Life in the village was very different from Litha Park, and I was teased by Mimi and the other village boys for being a 'city boy'. There were snakes that came out in the heat, and spiders bigger than anything I had seen in Khayelitsha. One day in the kitchen rondavel I screamed, '*Isigcawu!*' ('spider' in Xhosa) as I saw a massive spider on one of the pots. The boys found it hilarious and locked me in the rondavel with the spider. I was not stuck for long. I scrambled to the window and pulled myself out, much to the laughter of Mimi and his friends. I wiped myself off and walked away from their jeers.

Makulu kept chickens and pigs, and grew maize. I have a lasting memory of her pounding maize to make mielie meal, a stiff porridge and a staple in the diet of South Africans. In the Eastern Cape they have black pigs, and those pigs make the most delicious pork. Makulu decided to slaughter one of her pigs for us, and I had never eaten such sumptuous meat. As there were no fridges, all the meat needed to be eaten before it could decay. In Xhosa culture there is a term called *ubuntu*. It means compassion and humanity; we are one family so we share what we have. In the village, if anyone slaughters an animal they share it with their neighbours, who are more like relatives. People do not eat alone in the village, but each household takes it in turns to slaughter their pig or chickens.

Despite all the new experiences, when my father came to pick me up I was relieved. I was glad to go home to the comforts of electricity, proper roads and running water in Khayelitsha.

Back in Cape Town I saw my home with new eyes. I noticed the separation in the city: white people living in one area, coloureds in another and blacks in another. My father was not politically driven, and I never heard him speaking in anger about others. I learnt no bitterness from him, all he ever told me was that I needed to work hard. He knew that would be my only way to succeed in South Africa.

I knew my father loved me, but he never said it. Love was shown by giving. My father was not a man to show emotion. He was a tough village boy, and grew up without a father, as he had passed away when he was young. He told me as a man you must not cry, you have to be strong and tough.

3

No Education

One evening when we had just moved to Litha Park, my mother noticed a swelling behind my left ear.

'My boy, what is this?' she asked, pulling my head into her lap.

'Nothing, Mama,' I cried, as she prodded and pushed the area.

She inspected it and eventually asked Tata to check it too. I felt fine, but they agreed I must go to hospital.

The next day Mama took me to the Red Cross Hospital in Rondebosch. Again the doctors prodded and poked and said I would need an operation to remove a growth. To this day I have no idea what the problem was. My parents were uneducated and, even if the doctor had explained, my mother had not fully understood the situation.

I can't remember much of going under general anaesthetic, but they operated, and whatever they did was successful. I had to stay in the hospital to recover, and have my stitching removed and wound cleaned. I now have a long scar behind my ear, but nothing sinister was found.

I was on a ward with other children, and Mama stayed with me initially. When she had to go home, Tata would visit, and I remember lying in the hospital bed by the window, which looked out at the entrance of the hospital, waiting for him to come in his work truck to visit me. The only problem with this brief stay in hospital was that it delayed me enrolling in school, and I missed Grade One.

Eventually in January 1997, the year after we moved to Litha Park, I was put into Grade Two at Intshayelo Primary School. Because I had missed Grade One, I could not read or write, but I didn't admit it to anyone.

Each day I would walk with my brother, Vukile, the half mile to the school from my home and drop him off at the preschool next to Intshayelo. The school had yellow-brick classrooms, with red tiles on the roof, a parking lot, and a metre-high fence around the perimeter. We were around thirty pupils in each class, and we sat in pairs at desks. My two friends were Gift and Loyiso, and we would either play soccer or sit and draw together in the breaks. I loved drawing, especially cars.

I was able to hide my perceived weakness at school, by getting my classmates to help me with my work. My friends were smart, but some of them were very poor, and didn't have food, so I shared my lunch with them and they helped me with school work. I found the Xhosa language particularly hard to read and write. My friend, Gift, got me through writing in my Xhosa lessons by helping me in class. I never did my homework, as I didn't know how to study and my parents couldn't help me. As soon as I arrived home, I would throw my books down and try not to think of them again until I had to.

Despite not enjoying school, I loved my uniform. We wore grey trousers, a white shirt, navy jersey and navy-and-white tie. I was always the neatest child. I had black-leather school shoes, called 'Toughees', and I made sure mine were always clean and polished.

It was in class that I was first teased about my middle name, Shepherd. When the teacher did the register, he would call out my full name, 'Xolani Shepherd Pani'. The other children roared with laughter. *Umalusi* is 'shepherd' in Xhosa, and it means goat-herder, the lowest of the low. They would call, 'Hey, Shepherd!' mocking that I was a lowly goat-herder from the Eastern Cape. It made me ashamed of my name. Our teacher told them to be quiet, saying that Shepherd was a nice name, even quoting that Jesus was called the 'Good Shepherd', but I hated their jibes.

School finished for the day around 2 p.m. and I would go straight home because I had chores to do before my parents returned from work. Vukile was with me, and together we swept and tidied the house. Then I washed our white school shirts and socks in the bathtub so they were clean and fresh each day. I quite enjoyed the routine of it, and I loved being clean. We had no washing machine, so Mama would wash our other clothes in the bath at the weekend. Tata would then come home and, later, Mama at around 6.30 p.m.

When I got to Grade Six, aged twelve, I knew I would not be able to hide for much longer. In our Xhosa lesson, there was an oral section, and the teacher would call different pupils out to read in front of class. I knew if he called me, my failure to read would be discovered. Every day I woke up with anxiety, thinking, 'Eish, I hope today is not the day I will be called out.' It was a huge pressure on me, but I was too ashamed to ask for help.

Eventually the day that I dreaded came. I was sitting in class, trying to be as inconspicuous as possible.

'Xolani Shepherd Pani, come to the front to read to the class,' my Xhosa teacher commanded. We called him *Umfundisi*, which means 'Teacher'. I felt the prickle of panic rise through my body and sweat form on the palms of my hands. I wanted the ground to swallow me up. Rather than let the other children know that I could not read, I focused on the classroom door and ran for my life.

'What? You can't read? You are so stupid!' shouted my teacher, as my classmates laughed.

He tried to grab me, but I wriggled out of his hands, ran from the classroom and out of the school. I was devastated. I had no plan for what to do next, so my only choice was to go home. I cried all the way home, filled with shame and despair. Even though I didn't know God, my soul screamed: 'God, why did you let this happen to me?'

Mama was at home and I had to think of some reason to tell her why I was back so early. 'My teacher beat me,' I blurted out, sniffing and trying to wipe the tears from my cheeks.

She was immediately concerned, and took me by the shoulders, examining my face to see if I was hurt. I couldn't look her in the eyes. Mama wanted to go straight to school and find out what had happened. I could see my lie was about to get me into much more trouble, but I was able to convince her not to get involved.

The next day Mama made me return to school. I was terrified. Head bowed low, I didn't want to catch anyone's eye and face more teasing. Now both the pupils, my friends, and the teachers knew I could not read. Surely I would be ridiculed but, to my surprise, it blew over. My Xhosa teacher did not say anything more to me. No one helped me, and I did not ask for help. I was given no special care.

The following week in our morning school assembly we had a speaker. She was a Xhosa woman in her twenties. She said she was a social worker, and was there to tell of a new campaign to help children if they needed someone to talk to. She seemed so kind, and I was amazed there was a job where you could help people. The dream was placed in my heart to perhaps be a social worker myself one day.

I needed someone to talk to about my struggles with reading and writing, but despite her talk, and how warm the lady was, I didn't reach out, even though the opportunity was right there. To this day I don't know what stopped me, but maybe fear that perhaps I couldn't be helped?

Somehow I graduated Grade Six, and was pushed through to Grade Seven. This became a challenge, because the syllabus was getting harder, and I had a huge handicap to learning. I passed mathematics, because I could understand and read the numbers but, even though I could do maths, my maths teacher put me at the front of the class, as if I was naughty. My self-esteem was so low, I felt paranoid and was sure the Xhosa teacher had told everyone that I was useless.

I hated school and would wake up every morning telling my parents, 'I don't want to go!' My parents did not listen, not because they were unkind, but simply because there were no other options. I had to go to school.

The pain and frustration of not being able to read or write got to me eventually and in desperation I started to bunk off school. I would go to class in the morning, and then leave, after my third or fourth lesson, to go home early. I wasn't caught, and the teachers didn't seem to care, but as a result I was losing my only opportunity to learn.

4

Losing My Father

My father was not a drinker. The only time he would get drunk was when he went back to Butterworth alone every December to take part in ancestral ceremonies where alcohol would be consumed. However, when he returned to Litha Park in January 2000, he didn't stop drinking. I don't know what happened when he was back in the village but I assume, whatever it was was the cause of his drinking.

He had built his mother a brick house in Butterworth, and was seen as a success story by those in the village. The house was next to her cooking rondavel and he constructed eight rooms, but there was still no running water or electricity.

One Saturday in March 2000, a month after my eleventh birthday, Mama was working, and Tata was drunk. It was a hot day, and Vukile and I were at home with him. That afternoon Tata was going to a ceremony to slaughter a cow to thank the ancestors. Vukile wanted to go with him, but I saw Tata was drunk, and I didn't want to get in his *bakkie* (truck) with him driving in that state.

'Let me come, Tata!' Vukile cried. At 7 years old, he didn't understand the danger of Tata driving under the influence.

Thankfully, his pleas were ignored. Tata grunted, jumped into the driver's seat and placed a plastic bag of beers in the passenger seat next to him. He drove off with a skid of the tyres, down Hobohobo Street with Vukile running in tears behind him. There was no one else in the road and it was a hot afternoon; our neighbours were all resting in the shade. I called my brother to come inside. He was sniffing, tears still rolling down his cheeks, so I tried to make him feel better by suggesting we play video games.

Mama came home a few hours later, but Tata did not return. Mama and I sat waiting for him until it was late. Vukile was asleep already, and eventually Mama said, 'My boy, you go to sleep. Tata will be home soon.'

I reluctantly went to bed. The next morning I was still in bed when I heard the front door opening and Mama greet someone.

My bedroom door was open, and I heard a man say, '*Umfazi ka Mongezi* (wife of Mongezi), it is your husband, he was in a car accident.'

I sat up in bed, alert and scared. Mama must have been worried I could hear, as she quickly closed my bedroom door. Vukile was asleep, but I got up to listen more.

'It was a high-speed accident. You need to go to the hospital,' the man said. I recognized the voice as a friend of my father's.

I got out of bed at this point, and went out to the toilet so they could see I was awake.

Mama was shaking her head, her hand over her mouth. She turned to me and I saw the fear in her eyes.

'My boy, get Vukile up, we need to go to the hospital,' she said with a shaking voice.

'Yes, Mama.'

Vukile was grumpy at being woken, but we quickly dressed and left for the hospital.

I was thinking through what had happened the previous day, and the condition my father had been in. I told Mama, 'Eh, Tata was so drunk yesterday, I stopped Vukile from going with him.'

She shook her head and said quietly: 'You may have saved your brother's life.'

A minibus taxi took us to Groote Schuur Hospital. I was intimidated walking down the long white corridors of the hospital. We were told to wait on some plastic chairs, and my mother was taken to go and see Tata. I didn't want to go. When she returned, she was crying. Tata was in a coma and had severe injuries. We found out he had been asked to take people home to Langa township after the ancestral ceremony. He had been so drunk that he had crashed into another vehicle on the N2 highway. It was a miracle he survived, but others in the *bakkie* died. They too had been drunk from the ceremony.

Vukile would ask me when Tata was coming home. 'Soon, *Maraza* (Vukile's nickname), he will be back soon,' I would tell him, and give him a reassuring hug. We were very close, and I felt a responsibility to him, being his older brother.

Tata spent five months in Groote Schuur. Thankfully his work put him on sick pay, so we had some income. I was really scared of my father dying. Mama didn't cry in front of us after the initial shock, and I felt I should not cry too.

Tata was eventually released on 1 August 2000. He returned home with crutches, and Mama had to tend his injuries, cleaning his wounds, especially one on his back that took a long time to heal.

He eventually recovered, and was strong enough to return to work. He tried to pull himself back, but I could see it was hard. His *bakkie* had been a write-off and he had no insurance, so he began again to save bit by bit for a new vehicle.

When he had saved up enough to buy a second-hand Mazda car, he would drive me around Khayelitsha. One day we were going somewhere, and I headed for the passenger seat.

'Come this side,' Tata said, indicating the driver's seat.

I laughed, thinking he was joking, but he raised his eyebrows and motioned for me to get in the seat. With nervous excitement I obeyed, and jumped into the car. Tata explained the basics of the clutch and accelerator.

'When it comes to the clutch, move quickly, and then press the accelerator hard.'

I did what he told me, and the car jerked forward and stalled. It took a few more attempts until I could keep it going and drive on. After a few trips with Tata supervising me, I was allowed to drive alone to fill the tank with gas. The petrol station wasn't far, but it was still illegal for me to be driving at such a young age. I loved it. I felt like a king as I drove down the road. Other school kids saw me, and would run alongside the car. 'Xolani's driving! He's driving!' they shouted as I grinned, my head only just over the steering-wheel.

At the pumps I paid the R200 cash (approx. £10) Tata had given me for the petrol and then drove home. Our neighbours got very angry when they saw me.

'Eish, your boy will drive into our houses, or run us over,' they complained to Tata.

He just smiled and shook his head. He was a man with a severe stutter, and so avoided arguments whenever he could. He was also stubborn, and wasn't going to give in to the neighbours. Sometimes I would take Vukile with me on trips, and

Mama was never happy about it. 'You will get in trouble with the neighbours!' she cried, but Tata let us go.

Eventually our neighbours called a meeting, and Tata agreed to stop. I no longer drove in Litha Park but, when we were in a different area, he would let me jump in the driver's seat again.

During this time Tata's drinking got worse, and he would sit outside our house on the pavement with no shirt on, shouting and swearing. I was embarrassed by who he was becoming and I started being disrespectful towards him. I didn't say anything to his face, but would just ignore him if he asked me to do anything.

Before the drink, Tata would come home and prepare food for us. He had so much time for me. He would sit with me, telling me stories. I looked up to him. He was a strong man and commanded respect, but he was becoming a shadow of himself. He and Mama started arguing all the time about money, because he was wasting so much on alcohol. He only called for me when he wanted me to go to the shop to get more beer or cigarettes. I felt I was losing my father and I didn't know where to go with the pain I was holding. I heard my father's voice in my head, *never cry*. I was not able to speak about or understand my emotions. I just felt angry, and that anger began to grow.

5

'You Want to Smoke?'

In February 2002 I had just turned 13 years old, but looked younger as I was always a short kid. One hot and windy Saturday I was at home in Litha Park, and I was bored. Mama was working; she was now employed as a domestic worker for an Afrikaans family in Blouberg. Tata was drinking again, sitting outside in the shade of the doorway. Vukile was playing at his friend's, and I wanted to get out of the house.

I went out of the back door, so I didn't have to pass Tata, and swiftly ran out into the street before he could stop me. In reality I don't think he even noticed that I was gone. I decided to go a few houses down and see if Lucky was home, but before I got to his house, I saw Thulani, an older man in my neighbourhood, walking up the road.

'*Molo*, Tata,' I greeted him as I walked past. Calling an older man 'Tata' is a sign of respect in Xhosa culture.

'*Molo*, Xolani . . . Hey, come hang out,' he said, motioning for me to walk with him.

He was someone I looked up to. I was flattered he wanted to spend time with me. My decision to see if Lucky was home changed immediately. 'OK,' I said, quickening my steps to catch up with him.

I felt important walking with Thulani, and it was good to feel wanted. He asked me some questions about my life, and I loved the attention.

We walked at a gentle pace a little way from Hobohobo Street to an open field, surrounded by small houses. There was a large rock and we both sat down on it. I was wearing shorts and *takkies* (trainers) and a red T-shirt. It was a hot day, but the wind was refreshing. Thulani took a small bag of weed out of his pocket and started rolling a joint. I watched the procedure, interested in how he neatly rolled the dagga (cannabis) in the paper. I knew about cannabis, all the Rastafarians smoked it, but I had never seen the process of making a smoke close up.

Thulani glanced at me and laughed. '*Uyafuna ukutshaya?*' (You want to smoke?) he asked, waving the unfinished joint in my direction. I looked at him, and saw he was serious. He was offering me a joint! I liked him treating me as an equal, not a small boy. I wanted to be cool.

With a smile I didn't really understand, he lit the joint and handed it to me to puff. I imitated how he smoked, and breathed in the marijuana. Instead of a seamless inhale, I started coughing and spluttering. I stood up from the rock trying to catch my breath. Thulani laughed.

'No, not like that, you must do it like this,' he said, showing me how to inhale properly.

I got high that afternoon, and the sensation was amazing. I couldn't stop laughing, I felt so happy.

After a couple of hours, I went home. Mama was still at work, and Tata was passed out on his bed. Vukile was now back, so I brushed my teeth and sat down to watch TV with him. I had a huge grin on my face. Vukile side-eyed me, but he went on watching TV.

I went to sleep that night thinking about how I could maintain the feeling I had from the marijuana. I knew Rastas sold it, so a few days later I approached a guy called Jabulani who lived nearby, and asked if I could buy from him. He was only too happy to comply. Jabulani was a Rasta who thought weed was life; he didn't mind that I was a child, in fact he probably thought it was good for me. Tata gave me R5 each day to buy a snack after school, so that money went to my new habit. Five rand could buy you one smoke.

I got high at the weekends, and after school. I just ended up smiling a lot, feeling relaxed. It masked the pain of what was going on in my life. I hid the dagga and my lighter behind our garage at home, it was a space full of junk and my parents didn't go there.

Once or twice my father asked me to open my mouth so he could see inside – apparently you can see white on the tongue when someone has been smoking. He must have known the signs because he confronted me, but I denied it. Mama never said anything.

At primary school from Grade Seven my friend Loyiso and I smoked together. We found a loose face-brick on the outside of one of the school buildings and hid our weed and matches behind it. We called the area 'Sun City' as it was where the sun hit in the morning, warming us up from a cold night. It was just behind the toilets, and people walking past could see us smoking, but no one stopped us. This was my primary-school education.

My secondary-school experience was more of the same. I enrolled at Luhlaza Secondary School in January 2004, aged nearly 15. It was about a mile away and I walked alone on my first day with a certain amount of trepidation. I did not know how I would survive, still not being able to read or write. I had heard stories about high school – in particular, bullying from older kids. Luhlaza could be a rough place, and I was now a small fish in a big pond.

Even though I was apprehensive, I knew I looked good. Since I was young, my older brother, Lungile, had styled my hair like the black Americans we had seen on TV. It was short at the sides and he used some hair cream to make my tight Afro curls looser on top. I wore the school uniform of charcoal pants, navy socks and my Toughees shoes, a white shirt, tie and a navy tracksuit top with a yellow design on the shoulders. I cared about my presentation, and had a reputation for always being neat, looking sharp and smelling fresh.

I started Luhlaza with hopes to try harder and be focused. I dreamed I would find someone at high school to help me learn to read. I wanted to reach out to a teacher, but there was no one I felt comfortable to ask for help. In those days the teachers did not have the same training they have today. My efforts to try to be studious worked for the first few months, but by April I was bunking class again.

I didn't get involved in music or sport at school. I think the reason I avoided sport was I didn't want to have to change my uniform and mess up my clothes. Instead, I would go home, wash my white T-shirt, hang it up and then, when I had changed, I would play football or cricket with my friends in the street, or listen to music. My neighbour, Siya, was a year younger than me, and was into everything I was. We both loved house music and R & B, and would share our CDs. We would spend time at each other's houses listening to music. The South African musician, DJ Fresh, and Canadian DJ Glenn Lewis were our favourites.

Masibulele (who I called Masi) was a fellow pupil who was also in Grade Eight with me. Everyone said we looked like brothers as he had a similar hairstyle and the same dark skin tone. Masi was from E-section, an area close to the school. It was a chaotic place, and the kids were known to be naughty. Masi was no exception. Together we found a new 'Sun City' at high school. It was a place to smoke weed when we should have been in class. Masi introduced me to his friends, but they didn't like me at first, and called me a 'cheese boy' or 'mummy's boy' from Litha Park. I hated their bullying, and vowed to prove them wrong. I wanted to be tough.

At high school everyone started calling me 'X'. I was the X-man. At that time there was a Zulu hit song about the 'x' that cannot be solved, the unrestricted 'x', and people would sing the song when I walked past. It puffed me up and made me feel invincible.

Six months after I started high school, I came home one Friday to find Tata passed out drunk on his bed again. Mama and Vukile were out. As I walked into our kitchen, my eyes were drawn to the fridge. I could hear Tata's loud snores; I knew he wouldn't wake up. Quietly I opened the fridge and stole a few cans of beer. I went around the back of the house and drank until I was drunk myself. I didn't like the taste at first, but the feeling of being drunk was pleasant. I wasn't sick, and just slept it off. That was my first introduction to alcohol.

The cost for a two-litre bottle of cheap beer was R4.50. Masibulele and I and some other guys would buy the alcohol on weekends and pass the bottles around until we were all *unxilil* (drunk). There was no law at that time restricting sale of alcohol for those under 18, and if we were ever asked, we said we were buying for our parents and the beer was not for us.

My neighbour, Mandis, joined me in my drinking activities. He was born a year before me, but went to a different school. The pupils were white, Indian, coloured and black, so he had friends from all over the Cape Flats. He would tell me story after story of what he got up to, and I felt competitive with him, but not in a good way.

Masibulele and his friends often talked about guns. His brother was a well-known gangster in E-section. I wanted to be cool and accepted by them, so they would stop calling me a 'cheese boy', and it came to my mind that I could tell them I had a gun.

My father had a licensed firearm, a Norinco 9 mm pistol, and he kept it locked up in a safe he had built into the wall in his bedroom. He was from the generation that used firearms, and he said he needed it for protection. If he went out at night for cigarettes, he would sometimes take it with him.

Once while at work in Nyanga township he got into a fight with a taxi driver. For a time after the incident he would take the gun with him to work. He was very secretive about where he hid the key for the safe but, when he was drunk, he was not so careful. I saw him one evening as he got the key out of a bag in his wardrobe. He pulled out the black pistol, took out the cartridge and filled it with bullets. I watched as he stumbled outside, and started shooting into the sky.

'Eyyy! What are you doing?' shouted Mama, running for the door.

'Chasing away the witches!' Tata laughed, aiming at the stars in the night sky.

I laughed with him. I loved guns, and it was fun to shoot with my father. I wanted him to do it every evening, so my heart leapt a few days later, when Tata had the gun on him and he told me to join him outside. He put the gun in my hand. 'See, Xolani, I will show you how to use it.' He demonstrated how to take out the cartridge and clean the pistol. 'OK, you shoot something.'

Spreading my legs to brace myself, I held the pistol with both hands and then, holding my breath, I pulled the trigger. The bullet flew out of the pistol and ricocheted off the brick wall of the garage. Tata and I both started laughing. 'See, my boy, you can shoot,' he said proudly. It was a good memory with my father.

Soon my mother was calling me inside, 'This is not right, he is too little to be holding a gun,' she said crossly, but Tata just laughed.

To impress Masi, I decided I would 'borrow' my father's pistol and pretend it was mine. Waiting until I was home alone, I went into my parents' room and opened the wardrobe. I saw the bag on the floor, and shoved my hand in, scratching around until I found the key. My heart beating fast, I opened the safe. Inside was the pistol, lying on top of Tata's ID and other papers, with some bullets on the side. I took the gun, loaded it, and locked the safe. I hid it under my mattress in my room until I could take it out with me.

The next Saturday, Masi invited me to a party in E-section. It was a girl's twenty-first, and we would be gatecrashing. I took time getting ready and, when I knew my parents were out, I shoved the gun down the front of my jeans; my T-shirt covered it so no one would see. I ran out into the night, feeling bolder, but also self-conscious of the firearm in my possession. Ten minutes later I was at Masi's house, waiting for him to finish getting ready. When his mother was out of earshot, I told him I had brought my gun.

'Yoh, X! You have a gun?' he asked, surprised.

'Yah, I have a gun, but don't tell anyone,' I said nonchalantly. He still seemed to be amazed. 'How long have you had it?'

'Long time,' I said with a shrug of my shoulders.

Masi laughed, shaking his head. 'Eish, this is *news*!'

Lucky joined us and we walked over to the party near Masi's home. There was a tent attached to the front entrance and lots of people were crowding inside, drinking, and dancing to the loud music. In our culture, twenty-first birthdays for girls are a big deal, and families go all out, often going into debt for the party.

Since I had a gun on me, I felt extra confidence in the midst of the E-section boys. We had bought our own alcohol, and wanted to meet some girls. I danced with a girl I liked, and watched the DJ. It was my ambition to play music, and I loved the thought of being a DJ one day. About midnight the three of us decided it was time to go home. We had been drinking heavily, and we were all drunk and in high spirits. Lucky and I were going to walk Masi home, then we would go on to our homes.

As we were nearing Masi's house, we stopped in our tracks as we saw an older guy shouting at Masi's brother. They were fighting, and then his brother was able to get inside the house. The man started picking up big stones and throwing them at the windows of the house. The sound of glass shattering broke through the air.

'My mother is inside!' Masibulele said. 'Hey, X, give me your gun, I need to do something!'

'Eish,' I said, shaking my head, suddenly nervous. I wasn't too drunk to realize this was a terrible idea. I didn't want to give him Tata's gun, but I also saw the situation was bad. Masibulele's mum was vulnerable. In the end I pulled out the pistol from my jeans and passed it to my friend. I didn't think he would shoot, I thought he would just scare the guy but, in the darkness, Masibulele aimed and shot at the guy three times.

6

'X the Unstoppable'

It was all so quick, the peppered bite of the bullet flying through the air. Despite Masi being drunk, his aim was good and he shot the man's arm and then again in his leg. The guy fell to the ground, and I didn't know if he was dead. In a panic, I grabbed the gun from Masi and the three of us ran as fast as we could away from the scene of the crime. I sprinted between homes in the poorly lit township, trying to find a spot to hide. I heard the guy shout, so I knew we hadn't killed him. He had seen our faces. We were in trouble.

Lucky ran in a different direction, so Masi and I waited it out together, crouched behind a wooden fence, my T-shirt wet with sweat. We were on high alert, sensitive to any sound of someone coming after us, but nothing happened. In the darkness I could see the whites of Masi's eyes. He hiccupped loudly.

'Shhh,' I hissed.

'Sorry,' he mouthed.

Eventually tiredness began to pull at both of us.

'I'm going home,' Masi said.

I nodded, and let him slink off. I waited a few more minutes, and then made my own way home. Quietly I opened the back door with my key, listening to see if anyone was awake.

Mama had left a light on for me in the sitting-room. I turned it off, and in the darkness, hid the gun in my bedroom cupboard, before falling into bed.

The next morning I woke with a headache and dry mouth. I cringed as I remembered a bit of what had happened the night before. I immediately thought of Tata's gun; I had to get it back in the safe before anyone realized it was gone. I had slept late, and when I came out of my room, to my relief, no one was home, so I quickly put the pistol back in the safe, and then went back to bed.

I was nervous about going to school on Monday morning, in case anyone had heard what had happened. Seeing Masi at the school gate, he raised his eyebrows in greeting.

'You OK, X?'

'Eish, I think so, anyone know what happened?'

'No one, they won't know it was us,' he reassured me, but I was not convinced. I tried to keep a low profile, but Monday passed without a problem, as did Tuesday. I almost forgot what we had done. I assumed the guy Masi shot had not reported it. As Masi's brother was a gangster, maybe the guy was too and didn't want the police involved. I breathed a sigh of relief that I was off the hook.

However, on Wednesday afternoon, after second break, I was sitting in class when out of the window I saw the police enter the school gates. I remember thinking how strange that they were driving into the premises. It never crossed my mind that they were coming for me. A whisper travelled around the classroom, 'The police are here!'

We watched as the officers got out of their van and then walked towards the school building. A few minutes later, there was a knock on the classroom door, and my heart sank when I saw Masi walking with the policemen. We had been found out.

They came into the classroom, and Masi pointed to me at the back. He said, 'The police want the gun.'

The policeman looked surprised.

'This boy? Eish, he is so little. What is your name?' he asked.

The rest of the class were open-mouthed, watching the drama unfold.

'Xolani Pani,' I said, feeling the embarrassment of everyone looking at me.

'OK, Pani, give me your bag,' he demanded.

I handed it over and he searched it while I kept my eyes to the ground.

'Where is the gun?' he asked finally, throwing my bag back at me.

I could feel heat rising to my cheeks. 'It's not here,' I said.

'Well, you are going to show us where it is, come . . .' he commanded.

I stood up and followed the officers and Masibulele out of the classroom. I could sense the eyes of the whole school watching from the windows as we walked to the police van and Masi and I got in. I gave them directions to Hobohobo Street.

Mama was at home when we arrived. 'Xolani, what have you done?' she cried.

I just mumbled an apology.

'OK, where is it, boy?' asked the officer.

I showed the policeman the safe, and he took my dad's gun to check it was the one that had shot the guy. Masi and I were then escorted to Khayelitsha police station on Site B. Once at the station, they took our belts and shoelaces and then left us in a small cell with four other prisoners. One of the inmates asked what we were in for.

'I shot a guy with his gun,' Masi said.

'Yoh, you schoolboys have a gun? What are you doing with your life?' he said, tutting with disapproval. You know you are making mistakes in life, when even prisoners think you are foolish.

We were left alone by the other inmates, and that night as I slept on a urine-smelling mattress on the floor I wondered how I had got myself into this mess. We were offered a meal, pap (a coarsely ground maize porridge) and bread, but I wasn't hungry. I was so scared of going home and meeting Tata's wrath.

We were arrested on the Wednesday, and stayed in the cell until we had to appear at Khayelitsha magistrates' court on Friday morning. My parents and Masi's mother were there. We were wearing our school uniforms, but they were now grubby and dirty from two days in the cell.

To my relief we were released under parental guidance as we were minors, and sent home. I remember the walk with my parents back to Litha Park. We didn't speak; I could see my father was upset. My mother tried to ask why I did it. She convinced herself that I was badly influenced by Masi, but the truth was it was all my decision to steal the gun, Masi never asked me to do it.

When I got home, I bathed and washed my clothes, waiting for a beating or something, but although Tata was shocked, and I could see he was stressed by me, he did not beat me. I saw my parents' disappointment, but there was no punishment. In some ways I wish there had been, because in the end there were no consequences from stealing Tata's gun, and

Masi shooting the man. This just made me bolder as I realized I could get away with anything.

The following Monday I went back to school. I thought people would laugh at me, but what I didn't expect was their respect. No teacher reprimanded me; everyone looked at me in a new way. Girls I'd had a crush on in older grades started flirting with me. I could see them admiring me. I felt I really was 'X', the unstoppable, strutting around, feeling like the big man, not caring who I hurt.

Some of my classmates were not impressed though, the ones who were actually trying to learn at school, but I ignored them. I realized I could never be like them, because I could not read or write. Now I spent lessons smoking and drinking in the toilets with Masi and another guy we called Ayanda.

One time just after the shooting incident, I was smoking in the toilet when a pupil from an older grade came in. He wanted to take my smoke, but Ayanda said, 'Hey, bro, you don't want to mess with this boy.'

I looked at the older pupil and said with a snarl, 'You should listen to him, you don't know me.'

He shook his head, but left without taking my cigarette. I was becoming a tough guy, and I liked it.

Masi, Ayanda and I took chairs into the toilet so we could drink and smoke in comfort. The caretaker would come in, but he was scared of us, so let us be. We became more and more destructive and, because of my connection with Masibulele and Ayanda, I was meeting other guys with guns in Litha Park. We spent the weekends going to parties in taverns and mixing with gang members. I would sneak back in late at night, and fall asleep, but I was hardly ever home.

There was a gang house in our street and I spent lots of time there. Mama was so scared for me, and Tata tried to ban me from going, but I had lost respect for him, and ignored them both. I know I would never have dared to steal Tata's gun before he had the accident and started drinking all the time. I had also started taking his car out for drives when he was drunk. I would steal the keys and go for a joy-ride. He punished me if he found out, but sometimes he did not even realize I had taken the car.

Unsurprisingly I failed Grade Nine at Luhlaza Secondary School. At the end of the year, I went to my class to collect my report card. It informed me I had failed, but also there was a transfer note inside. I had to leave the school, and find somewhere else to finish my education. I saw the transfer as a chance for a new start, it was a glimmer of hope.

I had been living like a tough gangster, but really deep down I was just a boy, and I knew the path I was on wasn't a good one. I needed to change my friends, and I didn't like what I was doing. I thought if I went to a new school, I could start again, and have a chance for a better future. I wanted to get away from the learners and teachers at Luhlaza Secondary School. For some reason I had always found Xhosa difficult to read and write, even though I am Xhosa. I had taught myself English by watching TV, so I thought I would have a better chance with English. I asked Mama to take me to a coloured school, where they spoke and taught in English. My friend Umvuso from Hobohobo Street went to Vista High School, a coloured school in town, and he told me about Maitland High.

Mama took me to Maitland in January 2005 to see if they would accept me. We had to take the train, and it was a forty-minute journey from Litha Park to the school.

Mama was disappointed that I was doing so badly at school, but my parents were not educated people, and they trusted the school system to sort me out somehow. We arrived at Maitland and I had an interview with the headmaster, Mr Leon Kapp.

He glanced down at my damning report card, and then looked me direct in the eyes. 'What are you going to do differently if you come to Maitland?' he asked.

'Sir, I am going to learn, and I am going to come out the best,' I said, as convincingly as I could.

He nodded his head, as if pleased with the answer.

I was given a place to enter in Grade Nine, the year I had just failed. I was so happy and hoped this would give me a second chance.

My first day at Maitland High School I woke at 6 a.m., and put on my new uniform, a navy jersey and navy-and-white tie with charcoal trousers. As always what I looked like was important to me, and I made sure I had the charcoal pants, which were cooler than the grey option. Most of the guys wore grey trousers, but if you wanted to stand out and look 'top' you wore charcoal. I was out of the house by 6.30 a.m. to catch the train with other pupils from Khayelitsha.

I got to Maitland just before 8 a.m. and bought breakfast from the school tuckshop – a muffin and juice. I had made my lunch the night before – a white bread and baloney sandwich with an apple. I loved apples. My friends would laugh at me when I ate the whole thing, only leaving the stalk.

Going to Maitland felt so different from my previous school. The pupils were coloured, white, Xhosa and foreigners. I had two Congolese boys in my class. Many pupils were from the suburbs around Maitland, Salt River and Observatory, and they wanted to learn.

Mr Kapp, the head, was strict, and there was no way I would get away with drinking or smoking on the school property.

We did not study Xhosa at Maitland, which was the first relief for me. The school was made up of two campuses, junior and senior. I was on the junior campus to redo Grade Nine.

My first day I met a guy called Yanga, he was also a Xhosa boy, and he knew everyone in the school. We went to lunch together and he introduced me to the other Xhosa pupils from Gugulethu and Langa townships. Yanga was tough, and into some of the things I had hoped to get free from. But still, I wanted to impress him, and seem cool. I let him know I was friends with Masibulele, and some of his gangster friends from E-section. I was sharing the information for protection, so I would not be bullied.

I made another friend, Bongiwe, also from Khayelitsha. He impressed me, because he was very smart, and worked hard at school. He dressed well and was a lady's man. He would drink and smoke cigarettes, but only at the weekends. Bongiwe's friends had guns, but he did not let that life take away from being focused at school. He had older friends who were in professional jobs and they had a positive influence on him. He wanted to graduate and get a good job. I hung out with him, and got his help with my classwork. I was hoping there would be a teacher or someone I could confide in about my inability to read and write. When a stand-in teacher, Miss Brown, came to my class, I thought at last I had found a chance.

7

Cheese Boys

Miss Brown taught the life orientation class at Maitland, where we learnt about developing ourselves, democracy, human rights and career choices. She was a large coloured lady with short brown hair and she was always smiling. Her nature was so peaceful it made us all love her class. I was shy and quiet, having low self-esteem, so I didn't speak up, but I was growing in confidence in Miss Brown's class. She had a small CD-player on her desk, and encouraged us to bring our favourite music into her lessons, so we could have it playing quietly while we worked. Pupils were never disruptive in her lessons; we behaved ourselves because we all liked her.

Miss Brown had arrived at Maitland in May 2005, five months after I started at the school. As I sat in her class, listening to her talk, I felt I had finally found a teacher I could speak to about not being able to read and write. I tried to build up courage to stay behind after her lesson and ask her for help, but every day I found an excuse not to be vulnerable with her. Eventually, in September I decided that I was going to speak to her before the end of the week, but when I went to her class, she had an announcement.

'Learners, I have some news, I will be leaving in October, I'm going to the USA to study,' she said.

There was a collective moan of sadness from the class.

My heart sank because I knew now there was no point trying to speak to her. At the end of the lesson I left the classroom dejected. *You will never get anyone to help you, she was your last chance and you missed it*, came the angry voice in my head.

However, despite still not being able to read and write, I passed Grade Nine at Maitland. This was mainly down to getting marks for group work in lessons and exams being multichoice, and my guesswork being successful. I knew how to write my name, and I could figure out a few words, but in most exams I would sit in frustration, not being allowed to leave, and not understanding anything of what was being asked of me.

I went into Grade Ten in 2006, and at the same time there were more problems at home. I overheard my parents talking in stressed tones one evening. 'Someone has accused me of stealing diesel from the refuse trucks and selling it on,' Tata said.

'How can they say that? Why is this person doing this against you?' my mother asked, indignantly. Tata had gone back to work six months after his accident in 2000. For a few years he worked hard, until alcohol became a real problem.

My father was saying he had not done it, but didn't know how to prove it.

Tata went to a work hearing, and he was found guilty. There was a racket of diesel theft going on. He lost his job, but was given a severance package. With the money he bought a Mazda sedan. As there was now no income coming in, it was only a matter of time before my parents would have to sell our Litha Park home.

Going into Grade Ten was stretching, but I made a friend, a girl called Babalwa. She sat in front of me, was studious and focused, and the teachers loved her because she was smart and did her homework. Babalwa noticed I was struggling and took pity on me. I would ask for help, and she took time to explain things.

She was different from the other girls. They all wore their skirts short, but she didn't. They teased her for dressing like a granny but Babalwa wasn't bothered. She was beautiful, but I didn't want romance with her and to ruin our friendship. I knew what I was like with girls, and I didn't want to hurt her.

After getting arrested for having a gun when I was in Grade Eight I became popular with girls. Among my peers, there was pressure not to be a virgin, so when I was 15, I got drunk at a party and had sex for the first time.

My first introduction to sex was through porn. One evening I was watching late-night TV. Everyone was sleeping in the house when a pornographic programme came on ETV. I picked up the controls and made the TV quieter. I felt guilty at what I was watching, but also strangely drawn to it.

I was hungry to see more, and it wasn't long before I started watching porn on DVDs. It affected how I saw girls; they became objects to me, and when I was drunk I would do things I am ashamed of.

Each week I saved my pocket money to buy beer at the weekend. I was given R15 a day from Tata to buy food, and from it I would save about R50 a week for alcohol. At that time a can of beer was R6, so I could drink a lot on R50.

Now I was at Maitland High School, I tried to separate myself from Masi and the E-section guys. The shooting had caused a rift between us, and I wanted to have a fresh start.

At the weekends I spent more time with the boys I grew up with in Litha Park, like Umvuso, Siya and Lucky.

One Friday in November 2006 I was drinking as usual with my neighbour Umvuso, and two Sotho boys from Litha Park, Phumlani and Mabutu. I had dated Phumlani's cousin, and that is how I got to know him. He was my age, but a bit taller than me and with fairer skin. I liked him straight away, he seemed very friendly, and I wanted to impress him and make him like me. We chatted and I realized we were into the same things. Phumlani had a gun; it wasn't a licensed pistol like my father's, but it was also a 9 mm. I don't know how he got it, but because of the shooting incident it connected us and we became good friends.

That Friday in November, we were in a small tavern in Khayelitsha, next to a shop in someone's house, all drinking Amstel beer. Even though we were teenagers, we thought of ourselves as sophisticated men. We took care of our appearance, and did not want to be seen like the alcoholics, who got wasted on Black Label. People used to tease us and call us 'cheese boys'; when they did we would get up and act tough, as if we wanted a fight, but really we liked to be cheese boys.

I felt sharp in my Lacoste trainers, blue jeans and T-shirt tucked into my leather belt. My hair took about fifteen minutes to style in the morning. I would gel the top, brush the sides down before applying gel, and then I brushed it to create curly waves.

That Friday we returned home about midnight; Lucky wasn't with us this time. He often acted as my conscience, a big brother who cautioned me when I told him what I was getting into. If he came drinking with us, he would want to go home at about 9 p.m. I would walk back to our street with him, pretending to go to bed too, but I would watch from the window until he was home. I would then slip out into the night again, to find another party or shebeen to drink in. A shebeen is a township bar normally housed in a shack. When Lucky found out the next day what I had been up to, he was always cross with me.

'Why are you always going without me!' he said, but we both knew he would not approve of what I was doing.

The next afternoon, after we had slept off our hangovers at our homes, Phumlani, Umvuso, Mabutu and I decided to get food and alcohol at a place by Khayelitsha train station, where you could buy meat and beer at a good price.

I was walking ahead with Umvuso and Mabutu. Mabutu had Phumlani's gun on him, as he was wearing a jacket and could conceal it. Phumlani was walking behind with three girls he had just met. Phumlani was always a lady's man, and he was chatting with the girls, trying to persuade them to come with us. He was wearing a beanie on his head, it was his prized possession. Umvuso, Mabutu and I were in good spirits, looking forward to our beer. I noticed some guys walking towards us; they were a similar age, but I didn't recognize them.

The guys walked past us, but as they came to Phumlani and the girls, one of them grabbed the beanie from Phumlani's head, and walked off nonchalantly.

'Hey!' Phumlani shouted, and we all turned to see him clutching his head with no hat on it. Immediately the three of us retaliated, and ran after them, ready to fight. The guys were laughing at us.

'You think this is funny?' Mabutu said, taking out Phumlani's gun. He held it pointed to the ground. The atmosphere shifted.

'Where are you from?' he shouted.

'Harare,' one of the boys replied. Harare was an area of Khayelitsha like Litha Park.

'Go back home . . .' I shouted, but they laughed, until Mabutu fired a warning shot in the air. At that the guys ran, dropping the hat.

'Yoh! What just happened?!' Phumlani laughed, retrieving his beanie.

I felt like a gangster, and the girls were more interested in us too. There were no police around in Khayelitsha and we went on with our day, happy to have saved ourselves and the hat. What we did not realize was that one of the thieves recognized me, and knew where I lived. While we were still out drinking, they turned up on Hobohobo Street looking for me. When I went home at about 6 p.m. to get my jacket, as it was getting cold, my parents met me at the door.

'What have you done? Some boys from Harare came looking for you!' Tata shouted.

'Nothing, I don't know anyone from Harare,' I said, with a set jaw of defiance. They knew I was lying, but I didn't want to admit Phumlani had a gun and had shot it.

I went outside, to where Phumlani, Mabutu and Umvuso were waiting, and we stood by Tata's Mazda that was parked outside our house. We discussed what to do. I was angry and a little disturbed that those guys had come to my area. Mabutu still had the pistol, and we decided to go back to Phumlani's house as it was in a different area. As we were walking down Hobohobo Street, suddenly the Harare boys ran at us from a side street. It was an ambush and we were caught unawares; there were about four of them, and this time one of them had a gun.

I grabbed Phumlani's pistol from Mabutu and started running towards them, shooting randomly. Mabutu and Phumlani had ducked when the shooting started, but as they saw the Harare boys turn and run, they chased them with me. We got to an area of wasteland at the end of the street, and I caught one of the guys. He had tried to hide, but I grabbed him easily.

'What do you think you are doing? Do you think we are afraid of you?' I screamed, shoving the gun close to his face. I wasn't going to shoot him, but I wanted to scare him enough not to come back. As I was shouting at him, an old man came out of one of the houses near us. He called me by my father's clan name, Gaba:

'*Unyana ka Gaba* (son of Gaba), don't do that. We don't do that here,' he said sternly.

His words had an effect, and when Umvuso came running up to us, I let the boy go. My parents were in the street by this time, both looking panicked.

'Get inside the house now,' Tata commanded.

'You are going to start a war if you don't stop this right now,' Mama cried.

I was still sweating and full of adrenaline, but I followed my parents inside, noticing neighbours watching from their windows. The street had emptied at the sound of gunshots. Tata locked the door, and I sunk into the settee next to Vukile, who had been watching TV.

'What have you done? *What have you done?*' Tata muttered, pacing up and down. Eventually, as if he had made up his mind, he said firmly: 'We must get you out of here. You will die before you become a man at this rate.'

'Where can I go?' I asked, confused.

'I will take you to the bush for *ulwaluko*, your initiation ceremony, tomorrow.'

'Tomorrow?' Mama gasped. 'But he still has school!'

Vukile looked at me with wide eyes.

'It doesn't matter, our boy is trouble and he needs to become a man and leave his childish ways. He will bring trouble to us all if he stays here.'

Mama was silent, shaking her head in worry.

I could not believe what Tata was saying. This was not planned. I should have gone to have my initiation in the Eastern Cape years later, once I had matriculated. Tata was making a spur-of-the-moment decision, but my parents were obviously desperate. I swallowed hard at the thought of what was to come.

'Are you ready?' Tata asked.

'Yes,' I replied, wondering if I really had a choice. It would mean being circumcised in the bush, without pain medication. But what was the point of staying? I was failing school, and my life was going nowhere. Maybe this was the get-out I needed. Surely my life would get better once I became a man.

8

Life Unravelling

Before we left for Butterworth, Tata took me back to the sangoma in Nyanga township. I was nearly 18, so it was a long time since I had last gone as a young boy. Again we had to wait in line to see the old man. When it was our turn, we made our way to the shack behind the man's house. His silent authority was all as I remembered. Tata spoke to him first, and then I was called in to join them in the shack. As before the witch doctor made cuts to all my joint areas – elbows, knees and the back and front of my neck. As blood came out, he rubbed a black powder into the cuts, which stung. I winced, but made no sound, trying to be strong. He held my arm tighter and ignored my discomfort.

When a boy goes to the bush, the tradition is that the night before, he has a party with his friends. It is a ceremony to sing and drink, a final farewell to boyhood. My circumstances were not normal, and the trip was unplanned, but I still wanted my celebration.

'Can I have money to buy drink for my brothers?' I asked Tata as we travelled home from Nyanga.

He nodded, knowing what was expected, and gave me cash. He still had money from his severance package and, as he was also now unemployed, he had time to go with me up to Butterworth for the ceremony. Tata let me out of the house to go to the store and buy two cases of beer and two bottles of vodka, while he went to purchase our bus tickets for the journey the next day.

Since the age of 15 I had been to a few of these drinking ceremonies, before my friend's *ulwaluko*, so I knew what to expect. Everyone would eat first at their homes so I didn't need to get food.

I went out to the shop quickly, watching for the Harare boys, but they were nowhere to be seen. I knocked on Lucky's door and then Umvuso's, telling them what was happening.

'Bro, you are going to become a man, now we can be friends again!' Lucky said, patting me on the back. He had done the ceremony the year before, and so was supposed to hang out with other guys who had become men. I had seen less of him as a result. In Xhosa culture, the *ulwaluko* ceremony was both respected and feared. When a boy comes back from the bush a 'man', he is treated with deep respect. The ceremony happened mostly in June and December. It was still only November, so I would be going early.

Word got round to my friends and, that evening, one by one they came round to the house until there were ten of them celebrating with me. We started drinking, and soon I was put in the middle and they sang the songs that had been passed down from generation to generation, songs about leaving boyhood behind, and the new season of having become a man. I had been to Lucky's ceremony, and now we were all together singing the Xhosa songs about becoming a man. Everyone got wasted and I eventually went to bed early the next morning. When Tata shook me to wake me up, I was still drunk, but I had to get dressed and get to the bus.

'Are you sure you want to do this?' Mama asked. I could tell she thought it was too soon, she was worried for me.

'Yes, I am sure.'

I felt tired and hungover and I reeked of alcohol as our Inter Cape bus pulled onto the N2 from Cape Town. It was 4 p.m. on Sunday afternoon; so much had happened in the last twenty-four hours. Tata was silent next to me. I closed my eyes, hoping the journey would go fast. When I opened my eyes again it was dark. I had sobered up, and the full weight of where I was going hit me. I was scared.

'You see where we are?' Tata nudged me, motioning out of the window with his eyes. I didn't know where we were, we were passing farmlands and there was little light. 'We are far from Cape Town. Do you still want to do this?' he asked. I knew he wanted to see if I was brave enough to go through with it.

'Yes,' I replied, with fake confidence. I didn't want to show my father how I was feeling. I wanted to be tough, like him.

The bus stopped a few times for food and toilet breaks. Tata bought me a KFC meal and I hungrily ate the fried chicken pieces, cleaning my hands on a tissue afterwards. When we eventually arrived at Butterworth we took a clapped-out minibus taxi to Makulu's village, fifteen minutes away. It was early morning and there was a thick dew over the green plains. It was beautiful and, even though I was hungover, I appreciated the beauty of the landscape. We walked through the village to Makulu's house, and people soon recognized my father.

'*Molo! Kunjani!*' (Hello! How are you?) people called, asking if I was Tata's son, and remarking how old I looked.

Makulu lived in the house Tata had built for her, but still used the cooking rondavel. She had electricity in the house, and there was a tap for water in the village, so times had moved on since I was last there. It was good to see her again. She was very happy for me, and proud I was becoming a man.

The next day Tata got straight to organizing my ceremony. He explained to the elders what I had been involved in, and they approved that I become a man now. In Xhosa culture, when teenage boys are being naughty and rebellious, it is time for the ceremony, so that they will step up and be responsible.

I was nervous of being circumcised, as I had heard stories of the pain, but I realized it was too late now. I had told Tata I would do it, so I must be strong. I fixed my mind on the fact that I was going to do this at some point, so I might as well get it over and done with now. I told myself I would take the pain, and I would come through.

As is tradition, I needed another ceremony with all the boys of the village, so again Tata bought beers and whisky for us, and I spent most of the week drunk. Unlike me, Tata didn't drink at all, he was focused on the preparations. He went into Butterworth where he bought the blankets I would need, and found the right person to do the circumcision ceremony, and someone to stay with me in the bush.

I cannot speak much about the ceremony, as in Xhosa culture it is kept secret. But the following Monday, a week after we arrived in Butterworth, it was my time. I had the clothes on my body cut off me with scissors, and I was left naked, only covered by the blankets Tata had got me. The first week in the bush I ate uncooked maize meal, nothing else. The circumcision was performed that week, and my body was painted with white paste made from a rock.

I stayed in a grass hut made especially for me by men in the village, sleeping on the floor, and making my own fire.

One evening baboons tried to get into the hut, they were screaming and calling outside. I was terrified. I was a city boy, not used to the bush ways. Tata had given me a spear and we had a fire, but they were my only protection. I picked up the spear and stood waiting, but thankfully the baboons left, and I didn't come across any of the snakes that are in the area.

The circumcision healed well with no complications and after a month I walked out of the bush, a man. My mother and Vukile, who was now 13, had come up to Butterworth to celebrate with me. Tata slaughtered a goat and a sheep for the ceremony, to thank the ancestors. The men do the slaughtering in Xhosa culture, and then take the meat to the women who prepare it. There was lots of alcohol involved, especially *umqombothi*, the traditional home-made beer. I was relieved I had done it. It felt good to see my father boasting about me to his friends. I was happy I had made him proud, and I could feel our relationship being restored. I had passed a big test, but even though I was seen as a man, I still felt deep insecurity about my failure to succeed at school.

I left the next day with my mother and Vukile to go back to Cape Town. They now both treated me differently. Vukile would not be able to hang out with me any more; as I was a man we could not be friends. He would have to wash my dishes and prepare food for me if I asked.

I was now *amakrwala*, a man who has just been initiated. For six months *amakrwala* wear certain clothing to signify the change. I wore a smart suit, with a blazer and golf shirt, Carvela shoes, and a traditional head covering; some wear wide-brimmed straw caps, or flat hats, but I had a straw boater hat.

Back in Khayelitsha, I loved the feeling of walking down the road and being treated with respect by boys and other men, and receiving admiration from the women. There was pressure to 'test my manhood' on returning to Cape Town, and I complied, again becoming very promiscuous. I moved out of the house and into a space in my parents' garage. I could now host my friends and have girlfriends over. It signified not being under my parents' authority any more. As a man I could make my own decisions.

I wondered if the beef with the Harare boys would be over, after all it was more than a month since the shoot-out happened. A few days after I got back, I was walking down the street in Litha Park, and I saw one of the boys who had attacked us. I could see he was shocked at the clothes I was wearing, and what it meant. From that point on we never had trouble with the Harare boys; that is the amount of power and respect the initiation rite carries. The Harare gang knew they were still boys, so they would not dare attack me now that I was a man.

I was drunk on the power of it all, but in reality I was still a very immature young man. Back in my father's day, the ceremony was often done only for young men when they were in their early twenties, giving them a chance to gain a bit of wisdom before they were given such respect and honour from the community.

I, however, was not yet wise, and I came back to Cape Town to the news I had failed Grade Ten. It was no surprise. I had to redo the year. My first day back at school wearing my *amakrwala* outfit, I felt good receiving all the attention. It started on the train from Khayelitsha; all the pupils from other schools in town – Cape Town High, Rhodes and Seapoint High – all saw me, and I felt their respect.

When I got into my classroom the other learners all cheered me. My teacher said, 'Wow, you are a man now. Welcome to class, Mr Pani.'

Other classmates said I looked handsome, especially the girls, who get so excited when a boy becomes a man. Even though this felt good, my heart sank that I was redoing Grade Ten, while my friends moved on to Grade Eleven.

I saw Babalwa in the break time. 'Yoh, must I call you *ubhuti* (brother) now, not Xolani?' she laughed. *Ubhuti* is a sign of respect. I laughed, and told her she could call me what she liked.

I went to speak to my father after I had been back at Maitland for a few weeks. 'Let me work, I am a man now,' I said.

Tata shrugged his shoulders. 'It's your choice. It is true, you are a man now. It is time for you to decide.'

I felt a sense of relief and a weight lifted off my shoulders as I realized I was free from the torture of trying to learn. No more humiliation and frustration. I never went back to Maitland. I was free to enter the workforce, but with a failed Grade Ten, and no skills or experience, what could I do?

9

Getting a Job

To get a job, I needed a CV. This was difficult, as I could not read or write, and had no access to a computer or printer. However, a local guy, Luvuyo Rani, had recently opened an internet café named Silulo Ulutho Technologies in Khayelitsha Mall, next to Shoprite where we got our food. I found out that you could get CVs made there. I went in to enquire, and Luvuyo explained there was an online form to fill in and he would print it out. He asked my name, address, ID number and what grade I had finished at school, and typed it all into the computer. I was so relieved I did not have to do it myself. After a few minutes I walked out holding my new CV; it had cost me R5.

In the end it was my sister, Phumeza, who got me my first job in March 2007. I gave my CV in to the restaurant where she worked as a waitress in Tiger Valley Mall. On her recommendation, I got a job as a 'sculler', washing dishes. I was grateful for a way to make some money at last. Once you become a man, the expectation is that you now have responsibility to get a job, build a home, find a wife and father children to carry on the name of your father. It was a lot to take on as a just-turned 18-year-old.

Each morning I took two minibus taxis to work, first from Litha Park to Site C in Khayelitsha, and then another to Tiger Valley Mall in the northern suburbs of Cape Town.

I would sit in the taxi, with the other workers, and think, 'Wow, this is normal life, and it's not where I am supposed to be.' I never had aspirations to wash dishes, I still wanted to become a social worker, someone who was educated.

My first day at the restaurant I was shown the kitchen and my place at the dishwashing machine. I felt so down, so disappointed in myself. I felt I had failed in life, and I was embarrassed. As the week progressed the waitresses would complain a lot, especially when it was busy. They blamed me if things were not completely clean, even though it was the machine, not me, doing the cleaning.

My shifts at the restaurant were from 8 a.m. to 4 p.m. The whole day was spent filling the dishwasher and cleaning up. I was the only man working there and, although the waitresses were older than me, in their late twenties, they knew I was *amakrwala* and so flirted with me. I didn't enjoy the attention or the environment at the restaurant. The truth was, I had two girlfriends, and that was enough for me to handle. They were both from Litha Park, so I had to manage the relationships carefully as they didn't know about each other.

After three weeks at the restaurant, I started using my lunch-hour to try and find another job at the mall. With my CV, I went into Kauai – a healthy fast-food chain – and applied for a job. I came at the right time, as someone had just been fired, and they needed a replacement. I got the job straight away and promptly handed in my notice at the restaurant. So after a month as a sculler I was free. My father said my first month's salary should be given to him and Mama, to bring a blessing on my life. This is normal in our community, but often only if the family needs income. I received R1,500 (approx. £75) after my first month of full-time work, and dutifully brought it to my parents. Tata smiled when he saw me hand over the cash.

'I said, "Bring it to us" to see if you would obey. Now you can keep the money as you are a man. Do not drink it away, be sensible and save,' he advised.

I didn't listen to the last part of his advice, and spent a lot of my hard-earned cash on alcohol. Back then I wasn't good with money, not understanding its value, or the importance of saving. I bought clothes and new shoes with my first paycheque, and then gave some money towards the electricity in the house. That became my contribution to the household. I would pay for electricity, and bread if we needed it.

My first day at Kauai was a breath of fresh air after the restaurant. I was the youngest at 18, but the other employees were only a few years older. There was a fun vibe, and it was a nice environment to be in. I worked on the juice bar, making smoothies and coffees, and I liked it. There were other guys working with me, and it was a challenge to learn how to do everything.

I was trained on the job at Kauai, and given a uniform – a green shirt with a black apron. I wore my normal clothes to work, and then put the uniform on when I arrived. I didn't work at the till, as even though I could understand English, I wasn't confident in speaking to customers, and still felt a failure from my experience at school.

I loved making the smoothies. We had to be very careful not to waste ingredients, and I became an expert at including the exact amount of fruit, vegetable supplements and yoghurt or juice so there was no wastage. I was good at multitasking and worked fast. We had a manager, a white South African called Zoe, who came in to give training. She explained about the 'culture' of Kauai, and the different ingredients and recipes on the menu. Zoe was based at Centre Point in Milnerton, the Kauai headquarters. She championed me, and showed me favour in the job. She wanted to train me up to become a trainer myself.

I was happy at Kauai initially, but outside work, life was chaotic.

'You need to visit the sangoma,' Tata said one day when I was sharing my troubles with him. If things were not going well, Tata's knee-jerk reaction would be to see a sangoma to stop the bad luck. Tata still had the two belts on his arms filled with muti for protection. Now I was a man, I agreed that I probably needed protection too. In our culture we believed the muti could not only bring protection, but guidance and favour too. There was a lot of witchcraft around, and Tata was worried for me.

The following Saturday we went together to Nyanga to the same sangoma we had been to when I was a small boy, and just before I left to become a man. As I remembered, he didn't smile or chat; he was a quiet man and he beckoned my father into his backyard room to speak to him, while I sat and waited outside. They called me to go in a few minutes later. The dead baboon was still there, and I watched as the sangoma prepared the muti to go inside the belt. He cut the skin from a dead lizard, something like a Nile Monitor, and mixed it with black powder, which he then put in the belt. It was then placed on my left arm. He explained I must not wear the belt when I had sex with a woman, but always take it off.

Tata paid the sangoma and we left. At first it was uncomfortable having the belt on tight around my bicep, but I soon got used to it, and hoped it would bring me the protection I needed.

Tata's belts were obviously not bringing him favour, as my parents were struggling with money, so much so that they were having to sell our home, as they did not have the money for the monthly bond payment. They planned to move in with Cinci in Samora, and then try to find another house to buy as soon as possible. I hated having to pack up my things. This was the only home I had known, my friends lived on the same street, I knew the area and was known there. I didn't want to leave, but what could I do? I didn't fight, but I was angry, and silently showed my frustration.

When my parents eventually sold our Hobohobo Street house, with the money from the house sale my father bought a VW Trovit taxi. This was to be his new money-making scheme. Through links with my older brother, Lungile, he started a driving business, taking airport workers to and from the airport.

With our move to Samora, I asked Zoe if there might be a job closer to where I lived. She suggested a transfer to a Kauai in Claremont. So after a year at Tiger Valley, and a week's training at Centre Point, I moved to a new branch in the southern suburbs of Cape Town. I got on well with the manager, a man called Dion and, despite coming in late with a hangover more often than not, I was good at my job. I was promoted to training the new guys, showing the procedures of using the supplements and squeezing the juice. I would then supervise them for the first few weeks.

One pay day in March 2009, I decided to go into Adderley Street, in the CBD of Cape Town, and buy some clothes.

I still loved to look sharp, and I had my eye on some black suede Carvela loafers from a shop called Spitz. I went into the store, and picked up the shoes; they looked just as I imagined and, although they were R1,000, a lot of money, I knew I would feel great in them. I made my purchase, and then started walking toward the taxi rank to go home. On my way, I walked past the Central Library on Parade Street. For some reason, I decided to go inside, so instead of continuing to the taxi rank, I walked through the huge wooden doors into the building. Inside were rows and rows of bookshelves in a high-ceiling room. It was quiet, but the atmosphere peaceful. I stood looking up, with my mouth open, taking it all in, and not really knowing what I was looking for. I couldn't read, after all.

'Can I help you?' an older coloured guy asked.

'I am just looking around,' I said, hoping I was allowed to do so.

'Have you been here before?' he asked kindly.

I said no, and he explained to me how the library worked.

'You can get a library card and take out seven books or magazines, two DVDs and three audio tapes at a time,' he said.

At the mention of DVDs I was suddenly interested. I loved films, and this would be a way to watch for free. I signed up for a card, and I checked out *Coach Carter*. It was an American film, with Samuel L. Jackson. I didn't know the story, and couldn't read the blurb, but from the photos it appealed to me.

I looked around one final time before I left, and saw all the young people studiously working at desks, and on the computers. I felt a longing in my heart to be like them. There was quiet industry in the room, and all I wanted was to be able to join them and read a book and study. I wanted to learn and be successful. I wanted an education, but that ship had sailed for me.

I pushed the entrance door and walked out into the bright sunshine with my new shoes and borrowed DVD, but unable to acquire what I really wanted.

10

Near Death

In my hopelessness I did not know what else to do, but turn to alcohol. Getting the minibus taxi home from work in Claremont on Friday, I could hear the sounds of music coming from the taverns in Samora. Everyone was out on the streets having fun. I would drop my bag at home and then head straight out for a night of drinking with my friends. I was smoking about ten Dunhill Courtleigh cigarettes a day, but I didn't spend all my money on alcohol and cigarettes. I was wise enough to keep sufficient for my necessities: travel, airtime, food, my Dunhill aftershave. At the weekend I set aside about R200 for a night of drinking. The guys would get a round each, so R200 was enough for a round for me and my friends.

Most times when I woke up the next day with a painful hangover, I would think, 'Eish, I need to stop this cycle.' But I couldn't see another way. Peer pressure, my environment and lifestyle sucked me in. I wanted to please my friends, and it was my downfall. I was always aware that my life was not going well compared to my friends from Litha Park, like Lucky and Umvuso, and it made me feel even more hopeless.

After a year in Samora, we were overcrowding Cinci's home, so my parents found a place to move to, in Philippi. Vukile could stay as he was enrolled in school in Samora, and doing well. My parents were moving to a shack, and I said I wouldn't go. It was dangerous in Philippi and, after only a few weeks, some men tried to get in at night and broke down the door. Tata was able to fight them off, but they knew they could not stay.

Mama then found space in someone's yard in Gugulethu to build a home in. My parents purchased two wooden Wendy Houses, with zinc roofs, insulated with ceiling boards. The rent for the land was about R450 a month (approx. £25), but it was a stretch for my parents. There was electricity from the main house and my parents built one house for themselves and one for me, but I hated it. I had not been brought up in a shack, and the idea of living in one depressed me deeply. I spent one night in my badly built, cold, leaking new home, without plumbing, and that was enough, but I had nowhere else to go. I had to stay there in the week, but at the weekends I called up my friend Thando and asked if I could stay with him in Samora. I had made friends with him recently, after meeting through a mutual friend when we were out drinking in a shebeen.

At the end of 2009, after two years, I lost my job at Kauai, and it was my fault. I had started coming in late, and sometimes not at all, making some excuse or other. Dion gave me warnings, and he was very patient with me. He would have kept me on, if I hadn't started stealing.

A colleague showed me how you could take orders, but not put them through the till. I was never working on the till as I was still not confident enough, but if she was working and someone ordered a smoothie, paying cash, she would verbally tell me the order. I would then make the smoothie, and she would give it to the customer, without putting it on the system, where the order would be logged. She then shared the cash with me. I would never have come up with the idea myself, and stupidly I just went along with it.

There were a few of us doing it, and so we had each other's backs. It became a habit, and I became lazy, until one day another colleague told Dion what I was doing. He called me into the back office. 'Xolani, I have been told you've been stealing, not putting orders through the till. Is this true?' he asked.

'No, I would never do that!' I said.

Dion knew I was lying, but he gave me a break.

'I can either tell head office, and you will have to explain the R5,000 missing, or you can resign. Your choice,' he said.

I realized then I had to resign, because if head office found out, then Zoe would know. She had trusted and believed in me, and I didn't want to disappoint her. I took the hit for the others who were involved, and they kept their jobs. They were older than me and had children, and I figured they needed employment more than me at that point. I left Kauai ashamed of myself. It had been a good job, and I ruined it.

My fall-back was Tata's microbus business. My brother, Lungile, and I worked as drivers (even though I didn't have a driving licence or insurance), picking people up and taking them to work. But I was drinking and not focused. After work I would take the microbus to go and see different women. I often drove when I was drunk. It was as though I had stopped caring, and Tata could see I was risking my life.

One evening I pulled up at Cinci's house in Samora, and came into the house wreaking of alcohol. My father was in the sitting-room when I came in.

'*Molweni*, Tata,' I slurred, as I threw the car keys on the table.

'You are drunk,' he said in anger.

'Eish, not me, not your boy. Just a few beers . . .' I said, hoping to make it to my room to sleep.

'You are lying to me!' he said, standing up in frustration. Tata was never violent, and he didn't shout. As someone with a stammer he didn't use his words to fight, but he would often punish us through silence, sometimes not speaking to us for two days if he was unhappy about something.

I tried to avoid him, and fell into a chair. In my drunkenness I started to laugh.

This made Tata more upset. 'That car is going to kill you, I am taking it back to the dealership,' he said.

I tried to argue, I knew without the vehicle I would have no job, but Tata would not be moved.

By mid-2010 he had sold the microbus, and I had to look for other employment. I went job-hunting and found a vacancy as a barman at Caturra, a restaurant and café in Seapoint.

Tata and my mother made a plan that he would go back to Butterworth, and try to open a tavern. When it was up and running, Mama would go to join him. Tata was good at saving money, but he was not financially literate, and he misused the money back in the Eastern Cape. He ended up losing everything, even having to sell his *bakkie*, and came back to Cape Town by bus with his tail between his legs. It was really his drinking that was the problem. He had opened a tavern, but drank away his profits until he had nothing left.

Mama was just happy to have him back with her; she loved my father and was loyal to him.

My younger brother was very different from me. Always a hardworking quiet child, he devoted his time to school work, and took himself to church each Sunday. He did not go to Cinci's church, which was full of old people, but to a larger Pentecostal Assemblies of God. He used to leave his Bible on my bed. I knew he wanted me to read it, and was probably praying for me, but I wasn't interested. None of my family knew I could not read.

My father's health was not strong after his accident in 2000 and, with all his drinking, he was slowly killing himself. In October 2010 he called me over to the shack twice in one week. 'My boy, where is my *bakkie*?' he asked.

'Tata, you don't have a *bakkie*, you lost it in Eastern Cape, remember?' I said, confused.

'But what about the Mazda?'

'That has gone too, Tata,' I said.

He then went through every car he had owned, asking where it was. He was beginning to lose his mind, and he was only in his early fifties.

On Sunday 10 October I was at work on a day shift in Caturra when my cell phone buzzed from inside my pocket. I took it out and saw my sister Pamela was calling.

'*Molo*, sisi,' I said.

'Xolani, you need to come to Samora now,' she said.

'What is it?' I asked.

'Just come, quickly,' she said.

My heart sank, I knew something bad must have happened.

'OK,' I answered. In our culture we would never share the news of death over the phone, it has to be done in person. It was 3.30 p.m. I asked my boss to let me go early and he agreed.

I walked from Seapoint to catch the train to Philippi station. My phone had been ringing constantly with my mother and grandmother calling, asking me to come. When I eventually got to Cinci's all the family was there.

'We were waiting for you, Xolani. Your father has passed away,' Cinci said.

Tata had been in Lentegeur Hospital in Mitchells Plain since Wednesday when he had started to feel ill. He'd had a fatal heart attack and now he was gone. I hadn't visited him at all as I had been working. I couldn't believe he was actually dead. I told myself I needed to be strong. I didn't cry. I didn't want to accept it, so instead I said I needed a drink. I went straight out to the shebeen and got mind-numbingly drunk. I drank every day until he was buried.

A weight was added to my shoulders when my father died. I had to look after the family now, and this felt overwhelming to me as a young man. I felt responsible, and I had no idea how we would survive. We had no funeral policy, so no money to bury Tata. Even though my father had lost so much, he still found ways to make money, and that was all gone. In the end some cousins helped to pay for his funeral. The details are lost on me as I was just focused on drinking at the time.

The week after Tata's death was a time of mourning. The mourning cannot be held in a place that is rented, so we went to Cinci's home. Mama was wailing, devastated that the man she loved so deeply was gone. Despite his problems in later life, my parents loved each other and had a good marriage.

My job at Caturra was in the balance, as I was continuing to make bad choices. If I did a late shift, I would finish at midnight, and I would walk the four kilometres from Seapoint into town to go to the clubs on Long Street with my

Zimbabwean friend who also worked at the bar. A few times I bumped into the same Tanzanian guy, Marvin, who seemed to have a lot of cash. He was in his thirties and was a tall, slim man. We got talking and he asked me what I did.

'I'm a bartender, how about you?' I asked.

'I have a business . . .' he said.

'What is it?'

He looked at me, raised his eye-brows and smiled. 'You wanna know?'

'Sure,' I replied, now intrigued.

Marvin explained that he smuggled drugs from Brazil to South Africa. I was amazed, and asked lots of questions. I didn't care about the drugs, I was just interested in the good sums of cash he was making.

'What are the requirements to do your job? Can anyone do it?' I asked, knowing I had few qualifications.

'You need to be cool, and you need to be trustworthy,' he said.

We swapped numbers, and he told me to come and visit him in Guguletu. He was going away for a month, so he would get in touch when he was back.

In the time he was away I lost my job at Caturra. Sometimes the other bartenders and I would steal shots before going out after a shift. One evening I took it too far and stole a bottle of tequila. The boss found out and that was it. I was unemployed again. I had only been at Caturra for a month.

I was still living in Guglethu, and it was around this time that my muti belt from the sangoma fell off; it was worn down, but I had no money to go back to the sangoma. I didn't think much about it, I had other things to worry about.

One evening, Thabu, another friend, Kanye, and I were having a party in Samora. At 8 p.m. Thabu and I went to the taxi rank to pick up some girls we had invited. I had already had a few beers, and was in high spirits. We walked back to my friend's house, it was on the same road as Cinci's home. We were walking in two groups, and I saw a few guys coming towards us, but I didn't take much notice of them. Suddenly one of the guys pulled out a knife, and attempted to mug my friend who was a few metres in front of me. It was all so quick, my immediate reaction was to stop him, so I ran straight towards them to intervene. I tried to knock the knife out of his hand, and my friend was able to escape, but the guy stabbed me. I yelled in pain as the knife went into my chest.

I was desperately trying to find something to beat him off me, but I couldn't see anything. I could hear the girls screaming and crying, but no one was helping me. My younger brother, Vukile, had just stepped out of Cinci's house to go to the shops when he heard the commotion. He saw what was happening and realized it was me being attacked. 'Hey!' he shouted, and picked up a piece of wood, running at the guy. It was enough to get him off me, and my attacker ran off into the dark. I collapsed on the ground. I had been stabbed twice in the chest, once in my head, and once in my back.

'I can't breathe,' I said to Vukile, showing him the stabs on my chest. The knife had punctured my lungs, and I could feel my breath going out of the wounds. 'Press down,' I said with my last strength, hoping Vukile could stem the flow of blood, and close the holes. He took off his white T-shirt and pressed it against my chest. There was no time to wait for an ambulance, and no guarantee they would come to us in

Samora. Another friend got his car, and took me straight to G.F. Jooste Post-acute Hospital in Manenberg.

The doctors stitched me up, and I was awake the whole time. They gave me something to numb the pain, but I was still drunk so I didn't feel much. They had to shave off the hair on my head to treat the wound on my skull. After the operation I slept deeply, and when I woke up the next day they transferred me to Lentegeur Hospital in Mitchells Plain.

The doctor told me I had been very lucky. The knife had been so close to my spinal cord. He said they found I had some internal bleeding, and so had to put an intravenous pipe into the space between my ribs under my right arm. I was fully awake during the procedure, and the pain was excruciating, worse than the stabbing. But I was OK, it was miraculous I didn't die. If the wounds had been millimetres in a different direction, that could have been it for me. I was eventually discharged the following Thursday.

I was so angry when I got home. I blamed it all on having to leave Litha Park. Samora was an area of poverty, I wasn't known there, and it was dangerous.

'This would never have happened at Litha Park!' I complained to Mama. I didn't want to accept I was living in Gugulethu and Samora. 'My life isn't going anywhere, and it's because I live here now. Samora is a dark cloud over me,' I shouted.

Mama tried to make me feel better, but there was nothing she could say to change the situation, and I was not listening.

Being unemployed made me more interested in my Tanzanian friend's 'business'. When he got back from his travels, he contacted me, and I went to visit him in Guguletu. He obviously felt I was OK as he connected me to the big boss, another Tanzanian guy, named Edson. They both came to meet me in Samora one day, to see where I lived. Edson gave me more details of what I would be doing. I just felt excited. I would be travelling and making easy money, it seemed like a good idea.

'We need to wait until there is a trip, but in the meantime, you can get your passport, and your yellow fever jab,' Edson said. He gave me some money and I went to Home Affairs in town to apply and had my yellow fever jab at a private doctor in Athlone.

Getting the passport was a straightforward process, and a few weeks later I had my brand-new, navy-blue, South African passport in my hands. It was a ticket to adventure. I wasn't considering the danger, I just wanted to get out of Samora, and make some money.

I called my girlfriend – I only had one at this point – to let her know I had a job and I would be travelling for a few months.

'So you're gonna leave me?' she asked incredulously.

'Listen, I have an opportunity to travel, and get a better job. This will be good for us,' I cajoled.

'Why can't you just work here? Why do you need to travel?' She was suspicious, I think, wondering if I was just fobbing her off. When I eventually showed her my new passport and yellow fever jab certificate, she realized I was for real.

'OK, I am happy for you. I'll be waiting for you when you get back,' she said.

Her family were in a better situation financially than my own. She even had relatives living in Newlands, a rich suburb in Cape Town. We had been dating since 2009 and in some ways it was a good relationship. She was a student, so would only come and stay at weekends. She knew I had worked at Kauai, so I had let her believe I was still employed there. When she came over to Samora at the weekends, I wanted to impress her. I needed money to buy us takeaways to eat, and then give her pocket money to get home safely. I wanted to be the man and look after her, and this pressure to provide caused me to make more bad moves.

11

Brazil, 2011

My flight from Cape Town to Buenos Aires, Argentina, was at 9 a.m. on a Sunday morning in October 2011. I didn't need to get a taxi to the airport, as Marvin picked me up from outside the Samora library at 5.30 a.m. and dropped me off at Cape Town International.

After Tata died, Mama moved back in with Cinci, and I was staying in my older brother Lungile's room, as he was now in Gqeberha (East London). Before I left I downed a shot of whisky, to steady my nerves about flying. Mama and Cinci and my brother were all sleeping; I didn't want to wake them, and had said my goodbyes the night before. I told Mama I had a job with a South African film company on a movie set in Brazil. She nearly cried when I told her the news. She was so proud of me, she was telling the ladies in Samora her son was travelling. My lies and deceit were expanding.

It was still dark outside, and I picked up my bag, opened the gate and ran down the road to the library. Marvin's green Toyota Yaris was waiting in the street.

My main concern in flying had been the security X-ray machines that you go through at the airport to detect anything illegal on your body. I had seen them in films, and I wanted to make sure they could not pick up the drugs inside me when I came back. I was assured they could not. That was all I wanted to know.

When we arrived, Marvin handed me an envelope with $200 in cash for my expenses to get to Brazil by bus from Buenos Aires. It was a lot of money for me, and I opened my backpack to put it carefully inside.

'Good luck,' Marvin said, as I opened the car door to get out.

There was no script given to me about why I was going to Brazil, in case I was asked at customs. I had decided my cover was to be a DJ. I loved music, and if stopped I would say I wanted to learn about Brazilian music. If they asked whether the trip was 'pleasure or business', I would say pleasure.

Once I got through customs safely, I sat down for another drink, even though it was early morning. I looked at the other passengers, mostly foreigners returning home from their holidays. I wondered what people thought of me? Did I stand out?

The flight was nearly sixteen hours, and I was nervous but excited to be on an aeroplane for the first time. As we took off, I was a little uncomfortable with the feeling of the plane rising from the safety of solid ground, but as soon as we were up in the air I was OK. I asked an air-hostess how to start the TV screen in front of me, and put on the headphones to watch the films. From then on I was glued to the screen for hours.

Once we landed in Buenos Aires I was focused on following my instructions. I clutched a piece of paper with the name of the bus station I needed to get to. Outside it was a humid and cloudy day. I headed over to a taxi rank and showed my paper to the first guy I saw. He was a large man with a white T-shirt, and very friendly. 'Yes, I know where this is, I'll drive you!' he said in English, and I got into the cab.

As we left the airport and pulled onto the freeway I suddenly felt very far from home. First of all, the steering-wheel was on the left, which confused me at first. In Cape Town our freeways have three lanes, in Argentina there were many lanes and lots of traffic. 'Where am I? Please help me!' I internally prayed, in case there was a God.

After twenty minutes we drove off the freeway and pulled up at the bus station. I paid the driver in precious dollars, and I got out. I was tired and hot. I went to change my money as I had been instructed, and got on the correct bus for a two-day journey to my final destination. The bus ride was an eye-opener for me. We drove through the countryside of Uruguay and Paraguay, and I just stared out of the window. All I knew about Argentina was Diego Maradona and the football team. The city of Buenos Aires was beautiful but, as we moved to the countryside, to the villages and the farms, I was surprised at the deprivation I saw. I was shocked, realizing South Africa was not the only country with poverty problems.

Eventually the bus arrived in São Paulo. I went to a public phone and called my contact, Emmanuel. 'Hey, it's Xolani, I am in São Paulo,' I said.

He told me to get a taxi to the Hotel Republica. 'Have a shower and take a rest, and I will see you in the evening.'

I found the hotel and that evening met Emmanuel. He looked like a body-builder, a tall, muscular Tanzanian, and immaculately dressed.

'You look tired!' he said, laughing. 'Come, let's eat, that will make you feel better.'

Emmanuel took me to a restaurant not far away. It was a buffet and you could eat as much as you wanted. As we sat down with our plates full, waiters would come to the table with grilled meat that they carved onto our plates. I had no idea what meat it was, it could have been monkey for all I knew, but it tasted delicious.

We were just chatting, getting to know each other. Emmanuel was a 'caretaker' for people like me, the mules, who came in. He was fluent in Portuguese, as well as English, Swahili and Zulu. After a while we were joined by the head of the operation in Brazil, another Tanzanian called Bosi. He ate with us, and gave me instructions about what I must do. He told me not to tell anyone what my payment agreement was with them. 'That is your information, do not share it,' he said, and I nodded.

'It's good you have arrived safe, you are a brave man,' he said. 'This is Brazil, you will be looked after here. We are your brothers, you will be safe. We will let you know when you will travel back, so just relax for now. Get some rest and we will talk again.'

After the meal, Emmanuel showed me how to get a new SIM card, and where to go to use a public phone for cheap international calls at the Gallaria in the main square. I called Mama and my girlfriend, and then Emmanuel drove me to Boa Vista favela, and the house that would be my home for the next few months. Boa Vista was similar to Khayelitsha where I had grown up.

I was greeted by four housemates; with Emmanuel and me it made us six in the house. There was one other South African, a guy I called Rasta because of his dreadlocks. At 25 he was only a few years older than me.

'Welcome, bro!' he said and led me to a bedroom I would be sharing with him and a Tanzanian guy called James.

Emmanuel had his own room, and then there was an old Tanzanian guy, in his sixties, who I called Uncle. He shared a room with another older guy called Papa. They had both been in drug-smuggling for many years and had stories to tell.

There was one bathroom and kitchen, but the place was immaculate and well-ordered. Emmanuel was very neat and tidy, and we were all given chores to do in the house. We had to take a night a week to cook dinner. I would often cook with Rasta; we would make Brazilian yellow pap and veg with fish. All our food was provided for so we didn't have to buy anything. The environment in the house was clean and fun, you would never have guessed we were all part of a drug-smuggling operation. Women were never brought to the house, but the men would go off to visit prostitutes in the slum.

I learnt a lot about discipline from these men. In the morning at 7 a.m. they would all go off to the gym to work out. I eventually joined them, and week by week my physique started to change as I built muscle. The guys never took drugs, but we would often drink together. I became quite partial to a Brazilian beer called Brahma, and would drink with Rasta and James at the weekends.

James and Emmanuel had spent time in South Africa, but Papa and Uncle hadn't. I enjoyed talking about Cape Town and describing the beauty of the city. We spoke to each other in Zulu or English, but I started to learn a bit of Swahili, the language of Tanzania, as well as some Portuguese.

At the weekends we played football in a field in Boa Vista. There was a football club made up of Tanzanians, so it seemed every Tanzanian in Brazil came to the matches. Bosi would come with his children. He didn't live in Boa Vista, but in a nice apartment in a gated community house just outside the slum. He was a Muslim and family man. He did charity work and I remember he often justified what we did.

'Cocaine is a drug for the rich. Doctors and lawyers take it. It doesn't kill people.' I did agree that I hadn't, at that time, seen cocaine in the townships; there were plenty of other drugs, but not cocaine. Maybe it *was* a harmless drug for the rich?

'We are simply providing a resource,' he said, 'helping brothers get out of poverty.' I hoped what he said was true, and my fee for being a mule would help me get a foot up.

Every other week we were given 100 rias to go into town. Rasta and I would go together, buying bus tickets, and heading straight for the buffet restaurants. It was 15 rias for all you could eat, and we took advantage of it. As my cover was being a DJ, I visited music shops and went to different nightclubs to listen to the music. Deep House was my type of music, and the Brazilian style was a little different from what I was used to, but I liked it. I collected flyers of different DJs, and would always try and talk to them after a set. I didn't do any DJ-ing myself, but I was confident that, if I was questioned, I would have some good answers about the music scene in São Paulo.

Weeks turned into months and, before I knew it, I had been in Brazil for six months. We heard the cocaine had been held up in Columbia for some reason, and that is why it had taken so long. But the Tanzanians were patient men, and nothing felt rushed. I was having a great time, but I was also missing home and my girlfriend, so in March 2012 when Bosi came to our apartment and announced 'OK, guys, X-man is going', I was happy, but also daunted. My time had come; would I be able to go through with it?

Before I left I went to a *braai* at another house in the favela. It was in honour of a Zulu guy, who was visiting from South Africa. I got my food and sat down next to him.

'How are you, *bafou*?' he asked, using the traditional Zulu name for brother.

'Fine, fine,' I smiled.

'Ey, so you are from Khayelitsha?'

I nodded, wondering how he knew.

'Yes, I know your place. You live in Samora now . . . the house by the school.'

'How do you know?' I asked.

'Oh, we like to make sure we know about our guys,' he said, laughing. The conversation was jovial, but later I realized he was probably warning me. They knew I was about to make the trip and, if I had thoughts of running, I should think again.

The day of my departure, the cocaine was brought to our apartment in the favela. The guys were all there, having a *braai* and watching a football match. I had to focus on getting the black plastic bullets full of cocaine inside of me. Bosi took me to the kitchen where there was a bag of cocaine on the table. It was the size of a 250 gram bag of coffee. He and Emmanuel sat down and began to prepare the bullets for me to swallow. I sat and watched as they painstakingly rolled out the two-inch capsules in thin plastic.

Emmanuel explained that the raw ingredient would later get mixed with another substance before being sold on the open market. 'We have to be very detailed to make each one carefully, so it won't burst inside of you,' he said. 'Don't eat oily food when you have taken these, just a bit of bread.'

I could not imagine how they were going to get down my throat, it was overwhelming. When they had finished the preparations there was a pile of bullets for me to swallow. I started slowly, but then would retch and vomit, bringing one or two back up, so I had to start again. I felt sick, it was a mental battle, but Emmanuel kept encouraging me. Eventually, after three hours, I had swallowed them all. I lost count how many, but it was over 100. I was dizzy, and my stomach felt very full. I was relieved it was done, now I just had to get home safely.

Then it was time to go to the airport. After packing up my stuff, I said goodbye to the guys; we had become close over the last six months.

'Go well, bro, neh,' said Rasta shaking my hand. 'See you on the other side.'

'Be strong, and make the *money*!' said Uncle. Money was the motivation for all the guys.

My flight was 5 a.m. the next morning, so I was driven to Bosi's apartment to nap on his sofa for a few hours. Emmanuel came too. We had made a good connection and, as he had lived in Cape Town, I felt he understood me. Bosi had a maroon sedan; it wasn't a flashy car, none of the guys showed off their wealth, and they looked down on people who did. Their clothes were also simple – the equivalent of PicknPay instead of Prada – even though I knew they could afford Prada and much more. When they dropped me off at the airport, Emmanuel asked me to help find his son. He hadn't seen him for about fifteen years, after splitting with the boy's mother, but thought he lived in J-section in Khayelitsha. I promised him I would do my best.

I was flying from São Paulo to Doha and then on to Johannesburg. My stomach was fine the whole journey. I had a five-hour stopover in Doha, and was amazed to be in an Arab nation, seeing the men walking around in what looked to me like long white dresses. The airport was beautiful and opulent.

Arriving in Johannesburg, it felt good to be back on home turf. I was told people would come to get me. So when I came out of customs I was not surprised when two Pedi guys came up to me and greeted me in Zulu.

'*Ngiyabingelela mfowethu.*' (Greetings, my brother.)

'*Molweni,*' I replied in Xhosa.

'Are you Xolani Pani?' asked the taller of the two guys. I nodded. 'Come with us, please,' he said.

I had little choice, and so I followed them into the car park. We walked up to a shiny black, 7 Series BMW with darkened windows. One of the guys opened the door for me and I got in. I was a little unsure, not knowing where they would take me, but I had no choice. The driver introduced himself. He was another Tanzanian and he drove us out of the airport. The other two guys followed in another car.

We drove for a while, then changed cars and drove on to a very nice hotel in Pretoria. It was here I would stay until all the cocaine was out of my system.

'I need a Heineken,' I said, as I sat down in the main suite. What seemed like only a few minutes later a cold Heineken was delivered, with a plate of meat and pap. I ate and drank, and then just had to wait for my first bowel movement. I was given a bowl for when it happened. The raw cocaine was worth so much money and they were not taking any chances by letting me use a toilet.

A guy wearing surgical gloves came to take the cocaine that had come out and wash it off. I didn't have to do anything.

I was three days in the hotel, and on the Thursday they prepared my money. I was paid R85,000. Initially I was scared I would be robbed, so I went to deposit some of the money, and then kept the rest in cash. To celebrate my payment and the release of all the bullets, we went clubbing in Sunnyside in Pretoria. I was having a good time, dancing, drinking and meeting some girls. Even though I had a serious girlfriend, who I loved, I was not faithful to her. I had been constantly unfaithful in my relationships; it was all I knew.

On the Friday I went shopping at Markham department store and bought jeans, a wallet, a leather belt, a watch and shoes. It was March and winter was coming, so I also bought two thick jackets.

The next day I boarded my flight down to Cape Town.

12

'Why is My Life Like This?'

The sun was shining as I landed in Cape Town. I got a taxi from the airport to Samora, arriving at about 5 p.m. I let myself into the compound. The door to Cinci's house was closed; she was probably sleeping, and I did not want to disturb her. No one else was home so I put my bags in my outside room, and sat on my bed for a moment, letting out a huge sigh. I'd done it. It was now time to celebrate.

I called my girlfriend and arranged to meet her at a local tavern in a few hours' time. I then changed my clothes and, as no one was home, I went out to start drinking. It was an evening of celebration, and I was happy to be back with my girlfriend.

The next day I saw Mama, Cinci and Vukile. I was like the hero returning home, especially when I gave Mama R15,000 cash (approx. £750) from my drugs money. She had tears in her eyes.

'*Enkosi, unyana*,' she said. 'Thank you for working hard.'

I felt so good that I could help her. At last I was being a man, I thought.

My sister Phumeza lived in another building next to Cinci's house, and she came over to see me. She remarked on my new physique – from all the working out I had been doing in

Brazil. I now had larger muscles, and I had good intentions to keep going with the gym, but I never quite made it. The next few weeks involved a lot of spending. I bought a TV, DVDs, a fridge and a bed for my room at the back of Cinci's home. I was spending so much, feeling like I was a drug-dealer now, but there was no more money coming in. Soon it would run out, but I didn't want to think of that.

I kept in contact with the guys in Brazil through telephone calls. True to my word, I searched for Emmanuel's teenage son. It turned out that he was very easy to find, and after just one day I located the boy, and made contact. He and his mother were overwhelmed when I told them Emmanuel was alive and living in Brazil. They thought he was either dead or in Tanzania. I connected Emmanuel to them, and it felt good to do favours for my new friends.

But after a while my days became aimless, I had no drive to go out and look for work. I would sleep late most days, waking up around 11 a.m., and then go from my room outside to Cinci's house to see what food there was to eat. Usually I would fry some eggs in a pan to eat with bread. Once I had eaten breakfast I went back to my room to watch films or call my friends. With all my spending, it wasn't long before my money ran out and I had to find new ways to get money. I would ask Mama for cash for cigarettes, and Phumeza gave me some rands when she could.

My friend, Thando, was also unemployed at this point, so we were both needing to find ways to make money. One evening the two of us were walking home late from a tavern. We were both drunk but, as we passed a car parked down an unlit road, I had an idea. I knew about cars from my father and had seen that if you press a window down with force, a gap opens, and then you can try and open the lock. I pulled Thando's arm and, looking around to make sure no one was in the street, I went back to the car.

'Keep watch, I've got an idea,' I said.

I worked at the window while Thando stood a few metres away, looking out. Within minutes I was able to open the driver's door.

'What are you going to do?' Thando asked in a stage whisper.

'We can sell the parts of the car,' I replied, thinking on my feet.

I found a way to start the engine by fiddling with the wires, and Thando jumped in the passenger seat, shutting the door behind him. I knew we had to take the car to a different area, but where?

'What about Philippi?' Thando suggested.

It was a good call, as it was close to Samora, but another community. I drove off down the road, trying to find the lights and indicators. We left the car by a park in Philippi, and together took the four hubcaps off it, and a few other things from the interior, and then ran across the railway tracks to home. The next day I went round to a few mechanics I knew in Samora to see if they would buy what we had stolen. They were only too happy to accept the parts at my very discounted price.

Thando and I continued to steal parts and even cars from the suburbs. We found that we could use old car keys to unlock the steering-wheels, and then hot-wire the cars. We would then strip them down and sell the parts so we wouldn't be found with them. We stole about five cars in total, but we never sold the whole car, as I couldn't figure out how to do that without getting caught. We didn't get much for the parts, but it gave us some cash in hand, and that is what we needed.

I was also always on the lookout for an easy win. If I was at a party or at a shebeen and I noticed a drunk guy, I kept an eye on where he put his phone. If there was an opportunity, I would nick the phone, and sell it on as soon as possible. I didn't feel guilty for my dishonest behaviour. It was about survival and necessity, or so I told myself.

All this stealing was because I didn't want to be seen as a person without money. Thando was my closest friend at that time, and the only one who knew of all the criminal activity I was involved in. I was leading a double life, and this made me both stressed and depressed.

I told my girlfriend I was working at Kauai again. To keep the lie alive, I would sometimes tell her I couldn't see her as I was busy at work, even though in reality I was at home doing nothing. Lying was stressful, but I had got myself in the predicament, and I didn't see a way out.

One Tuesday night in September 2012, I went out drinking alone in a tavern close to Cinci's home in Samora. It wasn't the normal place I frequented, where there were people my age, but it was a cold night so I decided to go to this place close to home. I had a beanie and jacket on to stay warm and I ducked my head to enter the building. The shack was full of people drinking, slumped up against the makeshift walls. I ordered a Castle beer and found myself a seat next to an old, drunk guy. He smelt bad, and his eyes were barely open, but he held his beer bottle close to his chest and slugged from it every few minutes. As I sipped I looked around me in disgust. I was surrounded by lowlifes – people with no future.

'What am I doing here with these alcoholics?' I thought to myself. I downed my beer and ordered another, dark thoughts flooding my brain. I was hanging out with these hopeless cases, and I realized I was a hopeless case too.

When I finished my beer, I paid for a small shot of Bell's whisky in a bottle, and walked out into the night. It was drizzling, and I zipped up my coat to stay dry. It felt good to be out of that depressing environment, but the fresh air didn't lighten my mood.

As I walked, head down, my thoughts began to spiral, and I started weeping about my life. I never cried, but my level of depression was so deep. In that moment, I felt the only way out was to end my life. I was nearly home at this point and I stood outside the school opposite Cinci's home. Under a large tree, sheltering from the rain, I looked up and shouted into the dark night, 'God, where are you? Why is my life like this?'

Tears were streaming down my face, mixing with the rain from the sky. I heard no answer from God, so continued on home. I walked through the gate into Cinci's small compound, and unlocked the door to my outside room. I sat on the bed with the sound of the rain pounding on the metal roof, and decided to call Mama. I don't think I made much sense, as I was drunk.

'Xolani, what is wrong?' she asked when she heard my voice.

'Mama . . . I am sorry,' I said, starting to cry again. 'I have tried so hard, I'm so tired. I can't do this any more . . .'

She asked what had happened, but I couldn't tell her. Eventually I said I needed to go to sleep and said goodbye. She was babysitting in Claremont, so was staying the night there. Unknown to me, when I said goodbye, she phoned my younger brother, Vukile, who was next door in Cinci's house to tell him to check on me as she was worried.

When I put down the phone I started looked for anything I could take to end my life. I didn't know what I was looking for. The room used to belong to my older brother, Lungile, and I came across a bottle of his pills in a drawer. I don't know what they were, but I opened the lid, and swallowed them all, washing them down with the whisky. They knocked me out pretty fast and I have no recollection of what happened next.

I found out later that Vukile was knocking on my door, shouting at me to open up. He could see the lights were on and my music was blaring, but the door was locked, and I wasn't answering. In the end he kicked down the door to get to me, and found me lying passed out, with foam coming from my mouth. He was only 19 years old at the time, and it must have been terrifying to see me in such a state. He quickly called an ambulance, and I was taken to Groote Schuur Hospital.

I only woke up the next day, and found myself in a hospital bed, feeling very weak and nauseous. When I realized what had happened, I felt so ashamed. I was still miserable, but now I felt guilty too. I lay in the ward, watching the nurses come and go, dealing with the other patients, and I thought about my life. I had no money, but that wasn't the thing that depressed me. It was my lack of education. This was the root of my problem, and the reason I couldn't see a way out of my situation.

I was told a social worker was coming to see me, and for the first time I wondered if this would be someone who could help me. Surely they would do something, if I told them I couldn't read?

But I was disappointed. The social worker was a Xhosa guy, he spoke to me in English, and sat down with a sheet of paper. The only questions he asked were administration questions – my name, where I lived, date of birth, etc.

That was it. He never asked why I had tried to kill myself. I was so disillusioned. Even a social worker could not help me.

However, there was one nurse who was kind to me. She was a young Xhosa girl, a student nurse about 21 years old. My second night in the hospital she was on the night shift, and we started chatting. We talked about ourselves, and she asked why I had wanted to commit suicide. It was a relief to speak to her. As she was not connected to my life in any way, I opened up and spoke freely about my fears and depression. She encouraged me and was kind. I slept peacefully that night, and the next day I was discharged. No one had come to visit me, I think my mother was fed up with me, with my drinking and bad behaviour. I was relieved no one came, I didn't want anyone berating me for my decisions.

Once discharged, I caught a taxi van back to Samora. I was wearing the same clothes I had arrived in, and a jacket that my brother had thrown over me in the ambulance to stay warm. I didn't have my phone, as it had been left in my bedroom, so I couldn't tell anyone I was coming.

When I got back to Samora, I was nervous about seeing my family as I felt embarrassed and ashamed. Cinci was the only one at home when I arrived. She was in the sitting-room making clothes on her old sewing-machine. My grandmother was normally a tough lady, but she responded differently when I walked into the house.

'Xolani, my boy . . . Come sit down next to me,' she said.

I obeyed, and she took my hand in her gnarled and wrinkled hands. 'Why did you want to die?'

I just looked down and said nothing.

'If you continue living as you are, you will not live long. Stop this lifestyle, my boy. You have a good life ahead of you.'

I could see she was hurting from what I had done, and she really cared. She spoke to me with love, and it touched me, as it was so unusual for her to show affection. I couldn't answer her questions, and I just told her I was sorry, and that I was tired and needed to go to my room.

Phumeza came to see me later on. She sat on my bed, and tried to make me laugh. When it didn't work, she suggested something else.

'There is a revival meeting at the Ark of Glory church tomorrow. It's in the evening. I will go with you . . . Only God can help you now.'

I was wondering why she was telling me that, as she wasn't a Christian and didn't go to church. But I understood she was trying to help.

'OK,' I agreed. My friends and family, and even the hospital social worker could not help me. Church was my last resort; if God was real, maybe he could help?

13

'If You Help Me Get Back to South Africa, I Won't Do This Again'

Phumeza came to take me to the revival meeting the next afternoon. I had spent the morning lying in bed and watching films.

'Hey, Xolani, it's time to go,' she called through my window.

I sighed; I had little energy or motivation, but rolled my legs onto the floor and stood up. I changed into my black jeans, old Carvela shoes and a jacket over my sweatshirt to keep warm. There was a cold, north-westerly wind bringing rain to Cape Town.

It was about 6 p.m. as Phumeza and I walked into the community, and passed people selling their wares on the street, children playing, and mamas cooking over fires in their homes. As we got closer to the Samora library, I could hear loud singing, amplified by a sound system. The meeting had already started. When we got to the entrance of the building I was about to go through the open door, when Phumeza pulled my arm.

'I need to go and take care of something, Xolani, you go in and I'll meet you later,' she said.

'OK,' I said.

I went through the open door, the library was in front of me, and a community hall to the right. I had never been inside before and, as I walked in, I saw it was now packed with about three hundred people. There were no seats free, so when I noticed some people I knew from my street at the back, I went to stand near them.

A worship team was singing, led by a young lady on a microphone. I didn't know the songs, so I just listened, taking it all in. It was a new environment for me and I felt out of my comfort zone. I was worried someone would call me forward and pray for me, or expose me for being a bad person.

The pastor started preaching at 7 p.m., and he spoke for about two hours. I sat and listened, absorbing the atmosphere. I had nowhere else to be, and there was something peaceful and calming about the meeting.

As the sermon was coming to an end, the pastor began calling out things he felt God show him about the people in the room. Initially I was a little sceptical. He said there was a young woman in the congregation who was drinking a lot. The spirit of alcoholism had come from her community and had possessed her. As he said it, a young woman started manifesting a demon, screaming and shouting.

'Yoh! Evil spirits are real!' I thought to myself, glad I was quite far away from the girl.

I had never seen anything like it. At that point I didn't know about the Holy Spirit. The pastor started praying for the woman, and she screamed and writhed, until she was completely delivered and quiet. Her mother, an old mama, then testified that all the pastor had said about her daughter was true.

The pastor prayed for a few more people, and there was a call for anyone who wanted to give their life to Jesus Christ. I didn't really know what it meant, but I felt compelled to respond. My heart had been touched by the music and talk, and I had seen the power of God delivering the woman.

I waited as a large group of people went forward, and then I cautiously joined them. I felt embarrassed by the vulnerability I was showing in saying I wanted Christ, knowing my neighbours would see, but I was feeling convicted, and I knew I needed God.

The pastor prayed for each of us, and then some men from the church came to talk to me. They invited me back to the revival the following day.

'We also have a cell group on Tuesday evening, you should come to that,' one of them said. I nodded, and took down the address.

When I walked home at about 10 p.m. I felt a peace that was new. I felt clean, and I didn't want to do wrong again. But when I got to my room, and lay in my bed, I began to think of all it would mean for me to become a Christian. I would have to give up so much – sleeping with my girlfriend, my dishonest ways of making money . . . I wanted to know God, but I was worried of what others would say.

The next day Phumeza came to ask how the meeting had been.

'It was good. I am going back tonight at 6 p.m.,' I told her.

She raised her eyebrows and smiled, in relief, I think.

I was true to my word, and headed back to the library for the second night. This time I was more comfortable in the environment. I started singing along and clapping my hands in the worship. I carefully listened to what was said, trying to understand.

I went home when it finished, but as I walked to my house I could hear music blaring from the shebeens in our neighbourhood. I felt they were calling me.

I thought of my friends out drinking. I didn't want to be alone, so I decided I would go and see them. I needed to be with people, but I told myself I would only get a cool drink, and not have alcohol.

When I arrived at my local tavern I saw Thando and some other friends at a table. I ordered a Fanta and sat down with them. They were all drunk and laughing, having a great time. I was stone-cold sober, and I suddenly felt very uncomfortable. I didn't want to be there. What had once been my safe place and my outlet now felt foreign to me. I stayed for one drink, and then made my excuses and left. I was confused. The tavern was usually my happy place; now I felt I didn't belong anymore.

I pulled my jacket closer around me as there was a chill in the air, winter still trying to hold on to the mother city. Walking home through the chaotic township streets, I felt cold and despondent. I lit a cigarette and brushed my hand over my shaved head. I'd forgotten a hat, so I pulled my hood up and, eyes to the ground, kept walking.

As I kicked my feet along the rubbish-strewn roads, I thought of the dreams I'd had as a young boy. I wanted to help people, but that could never happen now.

The next morning I awoke when the September sun was already high in the sky. I lay looking up at my cracked bedroom ceiling. No one else was home, and I had nothing to do, so at about 2 p.m. I decided to go over to Thando's home.

Before I got to his house, I bought *vetkoek*s, purchasing the sweet fried dough cakes for one rand each from a vendor on his street. I was running out of cash, but Mama gave me what she could. The *vetkoek*s were still warm in the paper bag, and my stomach rumbled at their smell.

Thando was unemployed like me, but he had just applied for a job, so he had some options. I had none.

'Hey, bro,' I greeted him as he opened the door, passing him the bag of *vetkoeks*.

'X!' he said, immediately putting his hand into the bag.

We sat chatting for a while, and then put on a DVD to watch. Action and comedy were our go-tos, and we lounged on his old armchairs, drinking coke and eating the *vetkoeks*.

The film was halfway through when my Motorola phone buzzed. I flipped it open and read the message: 'Can we talk? Call when you have time.' It was Rasta from Brazil.

I sent a message back, 'Sure, call me.'

Within a few seconds my phone was ringing. I went outside to take the call.

'*Shom umfowethu*,' I greeted him (*umfowethu* is Zulu for 'brother').

'*Howzit, umfowethu*,' he said. 'It's been a while. I've got a deal – are you interested in making some cash?'

'Go on . . .' I said.

'My sister's fiancé is involved in an operation in São Paulo. We want to pull a deal off, and we need you to bring the coke back. If you can do it, we'll pay you R100,000.'

My heart flipped at the fee, but I didn't say yes straight away. Since going to the church conference, I wondered if there was another way to live. But then a loud voice spoke in my mind . . . 'Think of your brother, Vukile. You could pay his college fees, and you could buy yourself some suits so you can go to church . . . just do one last job.'

I went back inside.

'Who was that?' Thabu asked.

'Oh, just a friend, you don't know him . . .' I said. The fewer people who knew what I was considering, the better.

My thoughts went round and round in my head. Vukile had just matriculated and, as our father had died, I felt responsible for him. He was enrolled in Northlink College to study public management, and I wanted to help my mother with his expenses. I deceived myself into believing that my motives for taking the job were good. The reality was I desired material possessions, and the 'easy' money was too attractive.

Later that evening I decided to go along to the church cell group. It was in a lady's home near Cinci's. She knew me and my family and was overjoyed to see me arrive for the group, she must have heard I had been up to no good over the years. There were about ten of us, and the leader, Pastor John, opened in prayer. He was in his forties and from the Congo, but spoke in English. He opened the Bible and shared a word, but I didn't take much in, everything was all so new to me. We then started praying for others, and Pastor John asked what I wanted prayer for; I told him I needed a job. I said nothing about Rasta's offer.

The meeting finished about 8.30 p.m. and I walked home. I felt good being in the group, but I made up my mind. I would do one more job with Rasta, and then that was it. I sat with the decision for two days; part of me knew it was a bad idea, but eventually I called Rasta back.

'I'll do it,' I said.

I could sense his smile on the other end of the line. As I put the phone down, I prayed a silent prayer, to a God I didn't know yet, 'If you help me to get back to South Africa safely, I won't do this again.'

Once I said yes to Rasta, things moved fast. Within a week he came down to Cape Town from Johannesburg to collect me. I packed my belongings into a small black suitcase, and waited outside my grandmother's Samora home for him to arrive. Mama was at work, and only Phumeza was there to wave me off. I hadn't told her the truth of what I was doing, about being involved in drug-smuggling. I said I was just going to be delivering a package; I didn't explain that I would be swallowing the cocaine bullets, and becoming a human mule.

'I'm going with my friend to Jo-burg, we'll do the job, and then I'll be back,' I said.

'OK, *bhuti*, be safe,' Phumeza replied, giving me a hug.

'I'm always safe,' I joked, and she laughed. Phumeza was happy to be ignorant of the real facts of what I got up to. She didn't want to get involved in my stuff and she didn't fully understand the dangers.

I waved to her as Rasta and I walked down the road to the taxi rank to catch a ride into town. Rasta hadn't been to Cape Town before, so I showed him the CBD and where to have a good time at the Waterfront. It was great seeing an old friend and showing him my city, and it distracted me from the feeling of unease that had taken up habitation in the pit of my stomach.

After a few hours of sightseeing, we got on the Inter Cape bus back to Johannesburg for the nineteen-hour journey. Sitting next to each other as the bus travelled up the N1 to Three Sisters, then taking the N12 to Johannesburg, we talked about life, what we had been up to since we had last seen each other, money and girls – normal guy stuff. I don't know how Rasta felt about me, but I really liked the guy, and easily trusted him.

In the fading light, the green farmland and sleepy South African dorps (small country towns or villages) streamed past, and soon both of us were sleeping. After a few hours something woke me, maybe the discomfort of my head leaning on the window. I looked to my right and Rasta was still gently snoring on the aisle seat. It was now night, and I looked out of the window into the darkness, lights glittering in the distance from townships or cars. I swallowed hard. When you are quiet and alone, you think about your own stuff. I was afraid, and I felt something was wrong. Maybe it was conviction I was feeling, as on the previous trip to Brazil I had been excited, focused on getting the money. This time I felt sick, and wanted to get it over and done with. I closed my eyes and tried to sleep again.

We arrived at Park Station in Johannesburg at midday on Thursday, and Rasta took me to his sister's place in Yeoville, pointing out different places of interest in Jo-burg along the way. His sister's house was large and in a nice area. When we arrived she was very warm and friendly. She had a big personality, I could tell she was a hustler and a go-getter. Her boyfriend was Nigerian and older than she was. We all went out to eat at Mugg and Bean. I had a burger and chips, and we chatting in Zulu, but her boyfriend didn't speak much. I laughed a lot, acting relaxed. I was covering up, because I was still nervous, but I didn't want to show them. Rasta and his sister were party people, they always seemed to be happy and having fun, and it drew me in. I tried to forget my fears.

After our stomachs were full we went into the mall to get me some clothes. I would be flying to Brazil the next day, and I needed to look the part. What I was wearing was old and shabby.

'Come on, X-man, let's get you some nice things. You can choose,' Rasta's sister said, taking my arm.

I smiled at her and followed her into a shop where I picked out some burgundy *takkies*, navy jeans, a pink shirt and a black belt. Rasta paid for it all with his card.

That night the four of us partied at the Yeoville house. I was into Lil Wayne and Kanye West at that point, so their music was blaring out of the sound system. It was a vibe, and I drank and smoked along with Rasta and his sister, getting so drunk that I eventually passed out on my bed.

The next day I woke up with a hangover. The house was quiet, and I sat up, rubbing my face in my hands, trying to ease my headache and prepare myself mentally for what was to come.

Rasta drove me the twenty-five-minute journey to OR Tambo International Airport with his sister and her boyfriend in the car. When we arrived he handed me a package.

'This is $5,000 cash for Emmanuel – make sure it reaches him. And $1,000 for your expenses.'

I nodded, and put the money in my backpack. I'd never had so much money in my possession in my whole life. Rasta's sister and boyfriend stayed in the car, and Rasta helped me with my bag, walking me into the terminal.

'You know what to do, bro? We've gone through the plans enough?'

'Yes, I've got it,' I said.

'OK, tell the guys I miss them, and I'll come soon.'

Once he had shaken my hand and wished me luck, I was alone again, and trying to focus on what I had to do. This time I was flying SA Air direct to São Paulo, so I headed for their counter and tried to look confident.

When the plane landed in São Paulo over ten hours later the skies were full of clouds. In Cape Town when it gets cloudy it means the weather is cold. I was not used to this overcast heat. I took off my jacket, and went to the toilet in the airport to throw some water on my face. I then took a cab to a central area called República, focused around Praça da República, a lush square. It was a nightlife hub, but I wasn't going to be partying on this trip. I checked into the same hotel I had gone to last time, and slept there one night, as per Rasta's instructions. I was still feeling uncomfortable, but I had done this before, I knew what was expected. I just needed to keep my head down, stay out of trouble, and then get home. I decided I would seriously look into church when I was back in Cape Town.

The next day I took a cab to Boa Vista. Emmanuel was waiting for me as I got out of the cab.

'Hey, X-man! Welcome back!' he said, shaking my hand. He spoke to me in English and Zulu, which is very similar to Xhosa.

'Good to be back,' I smiled.

'You have something for me?' Emmanuel asked, as he led me towards the apartment building.

I nodded and once we were behind the wall of one of the buildings, I reached into my bag to give him the $5,000, wrapped up in an envelope. He smiled, approvingly.

We were staying in Flat 22 in a complex on a hill, overlooking the shacks in the favela below. There was parking and a football court in the middle of the complex. The flat had two bedrooms, so I had a room to myself.

The first night I lay in bed, with the familiar sounds of the favela all around me. It was hot, and I just had a sheet over me. I was tired from travelling, and when I closed my eyes I slept deeply. No dreams, just the sleep of the innocent, even though I was about to be guilty.

I now had to wait until my shipment was ready. Each day I would wake up, shower and go to buy bread at the local supermarket with the basic Portuguese I had picked up from my first trip. No one spoke English in the favela, it was only at the airports and at the hotels that I could communicate in English, so I had to learn the language. I remembered quite a bit from the previous year. I would go down to the football pitch to play ball and, if any of the locals were there, they would ask, '*De onde você é?*' (Where are you from?), and I replied, when I learnt how, '*Eu sou da África do Sul.*' People loved to hear I was from Africa, and asked questions about elephants and lions. I laughed, trying to explain I was just a city boy from Cape Town, I'd never even seen a lion. I learnt a lot in the favela, mainly that South Africa is not the only country with struggles.

When I had bought my bread in the morning, I would go home to eat breakfast, watch a film or play soccer and then maybe go into town. I didn't do much, I was still nervous and uncomfortable.

One day Jehovah's Witnesses came to the door. I had been hungry for some spiritual input, so I let them in. I wanted to learn about God, but I was also a little scared of what it would mean for my life. I knew his way must be the best, but how could I learn about him? When the Jehovah's Witnesses came I listened to them telling me about God, they spoke perfect English. I was aware something had changed in me as I never would have engaged with them before. I took their flyers, which were also in English but, as I was not able to read, I just looked at the pictures.

Emmanuel had a Bible and I asked to borrow it. Of course I couldn't read it, but I lay on my bed flicking through the pages, knowing I wanted to find God somehow. In my heart I prayed to the God I didn't know; I simply said '*uThixo*' (God) over and over, but I heard no answers.

The days were long, and I was eager to get home. I felt lonely on this trip. The previous year I had shared a room with Rasta, and we had had fun together. Now I did not feel like partying, and Emmanuel was out a lot. He used to travel the forty-five minutes into São Paulo from our apartment for meetings. When he shut the front door I would turn the TV on, or lie down in my room. I had a lot of time to contemplate my life, and my thinking was very negative. I am sure I had episodes of undiagnosed depression as a young man, and this felt like another such period.

I took solace in smoking, as somehow it calmed me. I could get through a packet of ten Stuyvesant cigarettes in an hour in Cape Town. When I first bought cigarettes in Brazil, I was shocked by their anti-smoking advertising. On the box was a photo of tar-lined lungs from smoking. The picture made me shudder, but it didn't stop me.

When I had been in Brazil a month, I was playing soccer with some of the guys I had met. Out of the corner of my eye, I saw Emmanuel coming down to the pitch. He beckoned me to come and, hot and sweaty from running after the ball, I ran over.

'Next week the tickets will be ready,' he said.

I nodded, understanding he was saying the shipment of cocaine had come through from Colombia, and it was time for me to fly home with the drugs inside me. I felt sick at the prospect, but also relieved that this meant I could go home and get my life back on track.

I packed my stuff; I had bought a fake Gucci sling bag and a few nice clothes for myself so my bag was full. I was ready.

Like the previous time, I faced a pile of cocaine bullets and, taking a deep breath, I started to swallow them one by one. After two hours my stomach was full and I was ready to go home.

14

My New Home

Landing in Johannesburg, I was so relieved. Six bullets had come out on the flight, and were now stored in my bag. I was just eager to get the deal over, and then move on with my life.

The cabin doors were opened and the passengers slowly snaked out of the plane. I placed my Gucci body bag over my head and through my arm, so it was resting on my chest. It was a relief to step out onto a jet bridge attaching us to the terminal. I followed the line of passengers and breathed in the smell of home; it was wonderful to be back in South Africa.

However, when I walked the few metres to the entrance of the airport, I saw there were three customs officials waiting. 'Ladies and gentlemen, if you have come from Brazil, please stand to the side here,' one of them said.

I complied, and stood waiting to see why I was being stopped. At this point I wasn't nervous at all, I never thought they would suspect me. Eventually all the passengers walked out through to the terminal. There were three of us left waiting: two South African women – they both looked Zulu – and me. I looked at the ladies and wondered if they were smuggling drugs; they were not dressed in expensive clothes, and could well have been mules like me. I never found out as we were separated straight away, and I was taken to an office by two customs officials, an older man with grey hair and a young guy.

'What is going on? Why are you taking me here? I need to catch a flight to Cape Town . . .' I said, trying to show them I was annoyed, and not happy with the treatment.

'It is just routine, Sir, we have to do these searches. We apologize for the inconvenience,' said the younger guy. He had initially greeted me in Pedi, although the dominant language in Johannesburg is Zulu. I understand Pedi, but don't speak it well, so I responded in Zulu.

The older officer's uniform was faded and worn, I could tell he had been in the job for many years. His colleague's clothes were fresh and new, the colour still bright, and he had the eager enthusiasm of someone new to their job.

After asking me a few questions, they took me down to the luggage carousel to wait for my bag. I pointed it out, and the older guy motioned for me to collect it. We then returned to the customs office.

By this time it was about 2 p.m. in the afternoon, and the office was quiet. The younger customs officer starting opening my suitcase on a large silver table.

'What do you do?' he asked, conversationally.

'I'm a DJ.'

'Oh, yes? What music do you play?'

I told him I loved house music, and we chatted about the music scene in Brazil. I showed him my CDs and he seemed interested, the conversation flowed easily. As we were talking, he was taking everything out of my case and systematically checking each item. He did not ask for my Gucci bag around my chest.

'Thank you for your cooperation,' he said finally, zipping up my bag and smiling at me.

'Am I free to go?' I asked, trying not to sound too eager.

The older guy, who had been standing nearby asked his colleague, 'Are you finished?'

'Yes, this gentleman has nothing illegal in his possession.'

I could not believe I was about to be let off, and the drugs resting against my beating chest were unfound. But I sensed the older officer was not happy. He looked me up and down and then asked, 'Did you search that bag?' pointing to my Gucci bag.

'Yes,' said the younger guy, obviously trying to cover up his mistake.

'Can I see?' the older officer said, and my heart sank. I had no choice but to give it to him. When he held it in his hands he was complimentary. 'Wow, this is a nice bag! Gucci, eh?'

I just smiled in a non-committal way.

He opened it and took out all my papers, ticket and passport. As soon as they were removed he saw the cocaine bullets at the bottom of the bag. He turned it upside down and threw them onto the metal counter.

'You said you'd checked!' he said angrily to the young guy.

The younger officer looked at me with contempt. I just put my head in my hands. I didn't know how I was going to get out of this.

I was left alone for a while, so I called Rasta. He picked up straight away. 'Where are you? I've been arrested,' I whispered.

'Don't worry, we'll make a plan to get you out,' he said, and then hung up.

I didn't hear anything else, so I called him again. He didn't pick up. I decided to try his sister. She answered straight away, and I explained what had happened. 'We'll make a plan, X-man. Don't stress, I'll call Rasta,' she said in a soothing voice.

When I tried to call her again, she never picked up. That was the last I heard from either of them.

While I still had time, I called my mother. 'Mama, it's me,' I said, with some trepidation.

'Xolani! Where are you? We haven't heard from you in days.'

'I'm OK, but I have something to tell you.' I paused, bracing myself. 'I have been arrested.'

'What! What happened? Are you OK, my boy?'

'Yes. But you remember I told you I was working in Brazil? It was not the film work I told you about . . . I was drug-trafficking.'

'Yoh! Are you serious? Why, Xolani?'

I apologized for letting her down. I told her not to tell anyone, and especially not my girlfriend. At that point I wondered if I might get let off, and then no one had to know.

I put the phone down with a heavy heart, just as the police officers came into the office. They were shocked when they saw me.

'What is this? Not this young guy?' said one, looking me up and down.

'You are so young! You are South African! Why are you doing this?' said another.

It reminded me of the time I was arrested for the shooting with Masi as a teenager. It felt the same, people didn't see me as a criminal, and they were shocked at what I was involved in.

I was handcuffed and driven with a detective and two policemen to a hospital in Kempton Park. They guessed that there would be more cocaine bullets inside me, and wanted to X-ray my torso to find out.

When we got to the hospital, two young nurses got me ready for the X-ray machine. One was Indian and the other coloured. I could tell they were nervous, thinking I was some dangerous criminal because of the police handcuffs. I just felt tired and confused, but I knew I couldn't fight this. If I was caught, I was caught. 'Let it be,' I thought to myself.

I sat down for the X-ray and watched the screen.

'What are they?' I asked the Indian nurse, as my insides appeared. There were what looked like lots of little black spots around my middle.

'It's the drugs. You are lucky to be alive, it's a very dangerous thing you have done,' she said.

I shook my head at the sight, aware of how vulnerable I was.

The detective who drove me back to the airport was a Zulu guy. He acted concerned. 'You are a young guy, you can say you were pressured to do this. I'll try to help you.'

He explained how they had a special toilet bowl made for this type of situation, and he suggested I try and keep some bullets back, to give to his colleague to make the sentence lighter. I just sighed; corruption was everywhere. It seemed everyone wanted a piece of the pie.

When we got back to the airport customs office they took off my handcuffs. For a moment I was alone, and I got down on my knees to pray.

'God, I accept this. Please forgive me and help me find you where I am going,' I prayed. It was my first genuine prayer.

As I had my face in my hands, and was on my knees, a lady customs officer came in and saw me.

'You'd better pray', she said, 'because you are going to prison for a *long* time.'

Her words didn't affect me, I had accepted my fate and my life was now in God's hands.

I was given a drink that would speed up my bowel movements and taken to a room with the special toilet in it. The toilet wasn't plumbed into the sewage pipes, but had a flush system to separate the cocaine bullets from my faeces.

I had been in the airport for a few hours by now, and I was hungry so I asked for food.

'You can buy some yourself, do you have money?' one of the customs guys asked. I had $300, so I gave him my smallest note, a $50 bill. About half an hour later I was delivered a chicken mayo sandwich, and a juice, but the man I had given the money to was nowhere to be seen.

'Where is my change?' I asked the person who gave me the food.

'There is no change.'

I shook my head in frustration, but what could I do?

I spent the night releasing the drugs, and sleeping on the cold, tile, office floor. I wasn't given a blanket or pillow, so used my jacket to lay my head on.

When all the bullets were out, I was taken to a police station in Kempton Park. I attended court the next day, and then was put on remand. It was November 2012, and my court date was March 2013. I would be on remand in Modderbee prison in Benoni. I was terrified.

On my way to prison, I knew I had to put on a tough exterior. I was not known in prison in Johannesburg, I had no contacts there, and I would have to stand up for myself. If I had to fight, I would fight. I knew prison was a place where people would take a chance if they saw you were weak.

My New Home

I had my luggage and my cigarettes with me. I was not given a prison uniform, as I was only on remand. If I was found guilty after my court date, I would then be moved to a different section of the prison and given prison clothes to wear.

I braced myself for what was to come. In the police cell I was safe. No one was going to harm me there, they would wait till prison where they could get away with it.

We arrived at Modderbee Correctional Services, about forty minutes from the centre of Johannesburg, at about 5 p.m. It was a huge, brown face-brick building, with a long, high wall surrounding it, and then another fence. As we got through the entrance, the van went down into an underground driveway to an area like a parking lot. All the prisoners had to get out of the van, strip off our clothes so we were naked, and squat two by two in rows. The guards then checked our mouths and made sure we weren't taking anything illegal in with us. It wasn't a nice experience, but I had no choice; I would be beaten if I didn't comply. When the wardens were satisfied, we could collect our clothes, but we were not allowed to put them on again until we were inside.

The prison officer receiving me took my belt and shoelaces and wrote down the details of all the money and belongings I had with me, so I could pick them up when I was released. I then put my clothes back on, and I was taken to my cell on the second floor and shown my mattress on the ground. There were no chairs or tables, just forty-three mattresses for the inmates with blankets and pillows, a TV on the wall at one end, and lockers where we could keep our things. At one end was a bathroom with a shower and two toilets in cubicles.

As soon as I arrived, if anyone looked as though they were coming towards me, I would death-stare them, so they didn't take a chance, or think I was an easy target because I was young. I scanned the men, looking for numbers on their arms, to signify they were members of the 26, 27 or 28 gang. The numbers gangs ruled many prisons in South Africa.

Khayelitsha's majority gang was the 28s. There had been many chances for me to be initiated as a teenager, but something always stopped me from going through with it. I hung out with the gang members in Litha Park and Samora, and my friends joined. Someone had once said to me, 'There is only one door into a gang, and the only door out is death.'

Because I was not a member of a gang, I did not come under any protection in prison, so I needed to be extra careful. Unknown to me, Modderbee had been working hard to strike out gang activity, and so it was probably the safest prison for me to be in.

The 'awaiting trial' part of the prison was named 'C-section'. We had a 5 a.m. wake-up when a prison officer coming on shift would turn on the lights to our cell. There was then an hour to wash. The cell was run by a 'cleaner', a fellow prisoner on remand who made sure we kept the cell tidy. Sean, the cleaner in our cell, was from the Tswana tribe. I learnt that he had been involved in hectic car-jackings on the outside.

At 6 a.m. we were counted. We had to stand by our beds, awake and alert, and a prison officer would check our beds. I imagine it was a little like being in the army. When the checks were done, the TV was turned on, and most of the prisoners watched TV until breakfast at 8 a.m.

We left the cell to go to another block for breakfast. I didn't have any friends, so I kept to myself as I ate my porridge and apple, and drank my tea. After breakfast the doors to the cells were opened and we could go outside for exercise. For the first few days I stayed inside the cell on my mattress, not speaking to anyone.

Eventually I realized it would be good to get some fresh air, so I walked around the field alone. In C-section we only mixed with other remand prisoners. The main prison was in another building and we never interacted with them.

There was a large field with high walls all around. Some men played football, others washed their clothes. We each had a bucket, and I paid someone R5 to do my clothes. It was a way of giving back, as you needed money in prison, and some people didn't have any. I had given the officers my dollars, and in exchange got prison tokens. They had five-, ten- and twenty-rand tokens, which was how you could pay for things.

At midday we came back inside and the 'shop' was opened, where we could buy soft drinks, tea, coffee and hot chocolate, biscuits (tennis biscuits were the most popular) as well as noodles. There was no lunch given by the prison, so money to buy food was important. At 3 p.m. we were locked back in the cell and at 4 p.m. six slices of bread, with peanut butter or jam and a boiled egg was delivered for each prisoner. We also had juice powder, which was added to water for a drink.

In the long afternoons in the cell we passed the time by playing cards, reading magazines or chatting. The atmosphere was generally good, although there were always petty fights breaking out between the men. The prisoners on remand hoped they might win their court case and leave. No one wanted to mess up that chance by bad behaviour. I learnt that if you had money, you could get whatever you wanted in prison – women, drugs, KFC – there was always a way if you had money.

Although all our phones had been taken away on arrival, many of the prisoners had mobiles smuggled in, and made their own chargers to go into the sockets. Prisoners would make calls from the bathroom, or from under their blankets. If you wanted to use someone's phone, you had to pay for airtime. The prison guards got paid on the fifteenth of the month, and were open to ways to supplement their income. In our cell there were both rich and poor, top intellectuals and people like me, who couldn't read or write.

15

My First Bible

I found out that C-section held church services for inmates on Saturday mornings. They were voluntary and led by people from outside. During the week an inmate had told me about Zion Christian Church and their service. He was very keen that I should go. I knew about ZCC as they are one of the largest African-initiated churches in South Africa. The men wear cream uniforms, hats with a star on and white shoes. Significantly, during the service they jump – a lot! I wasn't keen on jumping so I decided to try the other service held in the hall.

On my first Saturday in prison it was a windy day, but the sun was shining as I walked outside. We'd had breakfast and now it was free time. I could hear singing, and I realized church had already started, so I walked fast in the direction of the noise. As I got closer I could hear about thirty men worshipping in Zulu. Their voices were beautiful, but it was the words that touched me. It went like this:

Call: 'The sheep will know their shepherd and they hear his voice, and they know their Father.'
Congregation: 'We know our shepherd.'

I quietly took a seat among about twenty-five singing inmates and joined in with them.

After a while a Zulu guy in his thirties got up to preach. He introduced himself as Sabelo.

'*Bazalwane* (brothers) I greet you in the name of the Lord Jesus,' Sabelo said. 'I was once a prisoner like you, and was facing a life sentence. I was desperate, and prayed, asking God to help me get off. I said to God that if I got free, I would serve him completely. I vowed to come back to prison every Saturday to preach the gospel to the men awaiting trial like I had been. I was let off, and this is why I am here, to honour God and be faithful to my promise. I am here to declare to you that the Lord Jesus is telling you not to dwell on the past, he is doing a new thing in your life!'

I felt hope rise in my heart from his words. He preached on Isaiah 43:18–19. I remember it as if it was written in my heart:

> Forget the former things;
> > do not dwell on the past.
> See, I am doing a new thing!
> > Now it springs up; do you not perceive it?
> I am making a way in the wilderness
> > and streams in the wasteland.

Sabelo then shared more of his testimony, how he had been caught in a life of sin, but Jesus met him, and now he lived to serve and obey his Saviour. He spoke about God's love and his power to forgive. I listened to his words intently. I could feel my heart burning within me. This man was talking about a new start, and his testimony proved it was possible. I was aware of my bad past, I had done things I was ashamed of, and I wanted God to forgive me.

When Sabelo had finished preaching, he asked us, 'Who wants to accept Jesus as their Lord and Saviour?' It was a similar call to what I had experienced at the revival meeting in Samora. I wanted to go forward. I looked around; I would be going forward in front of my fellow prisoners, but they were all sinners like me. What did I have to lose? I knew I needed Jesus. I got up out of my chair and walked alone to where Sabelo was standing, I knelt down. Tears came to my eyes. For the first time in many years I wept.

'Brother, you can cry,' said Sabelo, his hand on my shoulder.

As he said it, it was as if the floodgates opened and I cried deeply. Sabelo prayed for me, and I felt as if I had been washed clean. It was the most wonderful experience.

After two hours the service ended. The officers were strict with time, and closed the meeting if it went over. Sabelo had to work to a strict timetable and we had to immediately return to the cells, so I could not talk to him about what had happened.

As I walked back, I felt so happy and free that for a brief moment I forgot I was in prison. It was as if I saw everything differently. The sky was so blue, I stared up at it in wonder. I saw a wild flower with delicate blue petals growing in the soil, and it was as if I had never seen a flower before – it was so beautiful. 'I want to know you, God, please teach me,' I prayed.

The following Tuesday we had our routine as usual. At around 11 a.m. I was inside the cell, while the other prisoners were outside. I hadn't yet joined them, but suddenly I felt compelled to go into the exercise field. I got up off my mattress, and walked into the corridor and down to the field. When I got out into the open I saw a tall, old, white man standing near the gate where the reception area was. He was at the opposite end of the field from where I was and he had a small trolley with him. I watched to see what would happen. He called over another inmate, said something to him, and then the prisoner shouted loudly: 'Free Bibles! Free Bibles!'

My heart started beating faster. 'Eish', I thought, 'I want a Bible, but if I go to get one everyone will see me getting a Bible and will all look at me.'

I had been putting a strong combative persona on for protection, and this would show weakness. However, wanting a Bible was stronger than the voice of fear. So, with shoulders back and head held high, I walked across the field to the man.

'Would you like a Bible?' he asked, with a smile. He had a kind face.

I nodded.

He asked for my name and wrote it down on a piece of paper.

'This is a Gideon Bible, so it's only the New Testament with Psalms in English, it doesn't have the Old Testament,' he said. He then opened it up and showed me the gospels, through to Revelation at the end. 'Bless you, my brother,' he said, and I walked back to the cell holding the word of God in my hands.

I was so excited, now I wouldn't be bored any more. I would try to learn to read, so I could understand Scripture and know God. I opened my new Bible and flicked through the pages, dreaming of the day I would be able to read its contents.

The next Saturday I went to Sabelo's church again, with my Gideon Bible proudly under my arm. After worship, he preached from Acts 12, the story of how Peter was arrested, and an angel released him from prison. I asked the guy next to me where the passage was in my Bible. He showed me, and I concentrated on it, pretending I could read the words.

Sabelo explained it was the power of the Holy Spirit that made Peter bold. He then shared about the disciples, how they were untrained and unschooled, but people were impressed with them:

> When they saw the courage of Peter and John and realized that they were unschooled, ordinary men, they were astonished and they took note that these men had been with Jesus.
>
> *Acts 4:13*

'They were uneducated like me!' I thought, and again it gave me hope.

When we were locked into the cell at 3 p.m. that day, I lay on my mattress and slept deeply. I woke up a few hours later. Most of the prisoners were also napping, or quietly playing cards or reading. I went into the bathroom with my Bible, so I could have some privacy. I sat down on an upturned bucket and, with the Bible clutched to my chest, I prayed, 'God, Sabelo was speaking about the Holy Spirit. If this Holy Spirit really exists, please help me to read the Bible so I can know you.'

A small whisper came to my heart, 'The way you trusted in the sangoma's muti belt, you need to trust in me, the God who made the mountains and the sea and everything in the world.'

I suddenly got it; I hadn't yet heard about Genesis, where God describes making the heavens and the earth, but he was telling me that was who he was, and I needed to trust him.

I prayed earnestly and from my heart, and then went back to my mattress to start reading. I began at Matthew. I decided instead of getting frustrated and annoyed that I didn't understand the words, I would take it word by word, write it out, and learn it, until I knew all the words. I had a supernatural drive, and a deep desire to know God. Hour by hour in the cell, my head would be in my new Bible. I found out that one of my cell mates had an English dictionary and I asked him to lend it to me so I could learn words I didn't understand. Over the next few weeks I got better at reading. It took me a long time, but I eventually was able to read about the birth of Jesus in Luke 1:35: 'The angel answered, "The Holy Spirit will come on you, and the power of the Most High will overshadow you. So the holy one to be born will be called the Son of God."' This blew my mind and made me even more interested in the Holy Spirit.

When Sabelo told the story of Peter delivered from prison, he was speaking about the boldness of Peter – who before was fearful, then with the Holy Spirit became bold to share the gospel. The people noticed Peter was uneducated and untrained, but his words had power and authority. I understood the importance of being filled with the Holy Spirit, and the things that hinder the Holy Spirit are: lying, jealousy, envy, sexual immorality, greed, etc. These things quench the Spirit.

Sabelo had explained our bodies are a temple of the Holy Spirit, and I knew smoking was unclean. Even though I was now a new man, I still had some habits I needed to break. Smoking was one. I would still smoke a pack of ten a day in the cell toilets, where all the other smokers were. Cigarettes were about R15 a packet then, and I was able to buy them with the money I still had from Brazil. I didn't want to continue this addiction, so I prayed for help.

I decided I would fast to break my habit. I had smoked since I was 15 years old. I didn't know about fasting then, that you can drink water, so I dry fasted – no food or liquids from Sunday to Tuesday. The Lord helped me, and I was constantly praying and reading the Bible. When I finished the fast, the desire to smoke was completely gone. I never wanted to smoke again after that.

Without being asked, before church the following Saturday I started cleaning the hall after breakfast. I was given a mop and bucket and I methodically washed the floor. I did not realize then that I was serving – and that serving our fellow brothers is an important principle of the Christian faith. I just felt compelled to do it. Later I read in Mark 10:45: 'For even the Son of Man did not come to be served but to serve.' And I understood that Jesus was the ultimate servant.

There were three phone booths in each section with Telkom lines that we could use to call out at weekends. I called my mother every Saturday, waiting in line until a phone was free. After my money from Brazil ran out, the way I survived in prison was to sell Telkom cards. I would get Mama to buy me R100 and R50 Telkom vouchers. I then sold them on at a higher price, and so was able to pay for washing clothes, haircuts and buying extra clothes. Because of my constant Bible reading, I was seen as a pastor, and I wanted to look the part. From childhood I had made sure I was clean and tidy, smelling good with aftershave and deodorant.

Day by day I studied my Bible. When I got to the Beatitudes in Matthew 5, I was really touched by the words of Jesus. Matthew 5:5 says 'Blessed are the meek, for they will inherit the earth.' I didn't know what 'meek' meant, so I checked the dictionary. It was about having a modest opinion of your own importance, being humble. I prayed, asking for this gift, to be humble. I saw that Jesus, even though he was God, walked in humility, and I wanted to emulate him.

A few weeks later I got to the crucifixion and death of Jesus in Matthew 27. It took me three weeks to read the whole story and I couldn't believe what I was reading. *How could they kill him?* I understood that Pontius Pilate found him innocent, but the other guys, the Pharisees, said he was evil. I didn't understand why they would do that.

Growing up I had always dreamed of a world of peace and love, but I saw people around me hated each other. The world was full of wars and violence. When I read about the life of Jesus, I saw he was bringing love wherever he went. He was the answer to the world I had dreamed about, but they crucified him. As I read the passage of his death, I wept.

I was sitting on my mattress, with my back against the wall and I dropped my Bible into my lap in shock. Looking around the cell, some of the prisoners were sleeping but others were playing cards and could see I was crying. I took my bedsheet and put it over my head to hide the tears flowing down my cheeks. *How could they kill him?*

Eventually I continued reading, and when I got to the bit where Jesus rose again, I was so happy! Jesus defeated death, and is alive! I was deeply relieved. I then read about Jesus appearing to Mary, and telling her he was not glorified yet, but must go to the Father. I just thought, 'Wow, God is so beautiful!'

Since arriving at prison I had been called Shepherd, my middle name, even by my fellow Xhosa and Zulu prisoners, who could read that on my prison card (which we had to have on us at all times) my first name was Xolani.

The more I got to read the Bible I saw how God changes names – Saul to Paul, and the disciple Simon to Peter which means 'rock'. I knew that Xolani was the name of my past, the past I was ashamed of. I was beginning to see 'shepherd' again and again in the Bible. I needed a new name that would bring glory to God and I felt God say he was making me a shepherd, and my name was prophetic. From that point on I embraced my new name.

Week by week, adding to my Bible reading was the teaching from Sabelo at church. He helped me have a deeper understanding of different Scriptures. Sabelo explained what it means to be born again from John 3. The Pharisee, Nicodemus, asks what Jesus means when he says no one can see the kingdom of God unless they are born again:

> 'How can someone be born when they are old?' Nicodemus asked. 'Surely they cannot enter a second time into their mother's womb to be born!'
>
> Jesus answered, 'Very truly I tell you, no one can enter the kingdom of God unless they are born of water and the Spirit.'
>
> *John 3:4–5*

Now I was filled with the Spirit, I was born again, and I went around telling my fellow prisoners that they needed to be saved.

My deliverance from lust, rejection, idolatry, and other sin that I knew had been energized by the demonic, was not dramatic, as I had already been set free by the word of God. When I started to read the Bible, I would feel a heat on my stomach as I read. When I stopped, it went, and when I read again, it returned. It confused me until I realized the word of God was cleaning me from the inside out. Psalm 107:20 says: 'He sent out his word and healed them.' Jesus prayed in John 17:17: 'Sanctify them by the truth; your word is truth.' And Matthew 6:22 says: 'The eye is the lamp of the body.'

Whatever you are letting in through your eyes affects your whole body. Whenever I read Scriptures I felt a supernatural manifestation in my body – I would even get hot hands at the wrist. When I felt weak, Scripture energized me.

By February 2013 my court date was looming. It was assumed I would plead not guilty but, after reading the Bible and becoming a Christian, I knew I could not lie. I told a few of the inmates, and they said I was crazy. I could possibly get off for being young, claiming I was forced to do it. But I knew that would be dishonest. I was now born again, and I could not lie. I had to face my wrongdoing.

The day of my court case was 10 April 2013. It was an unusually cloudy day, and I put on my smartest clothes – the pink shirt and blue jeans bought for me by Rasta to fly to Brazil. I had paid for them to be washed and ironed by a fellow inmate. There was one iron available to us prisoners, but there were tight rules about using it. You could only iron clothes in the kitchen, and with the iron you took a card, which explained you had full responsibility for it. The guards knew it could be a nasty weapon if in the wrong hands.

There were six of us going for sentencing that day. There was no emotional goodbye to the other inmates, as we didn't know if we would be back later in the day.

We were let out early in the morning and taken to reception to get our possessions. It was good to have my phone again, but I realized it was dead, and I had no way to charge it, so I took out the SIM card, and used a fellow prisoner's phone to call Mama.

'I'm on my way to court, and I will let you know the verdict,' I said; I didn't want to say too much to stress her out.

I also tried to call Rasta, but there was no answer. As we waited I spoke to a homeless man who had been arrested and was waiting to be processed. I told him Jesus was his only hope; he nodded.

Once I had everything, we were driven in a police van with an escort, sirens blaring, to the court in Kempton Park. I felt downcast at the mess I had made of my life. I looked out of the window at the brown Johannesburg landscape speeding past, and felt very far from home. It was still early when we arrived, and we were given porridge and tea for breakfast. As I sat waiting for my time, I just kept praying: 'Lord, I am trusting you, no matter the outcome. I can't deny that I did what I did. I want to be an honest man from this moment on.'

Someone came to ask me if I had a legal representative. I said no and they asked if I wanted a state lawyer. I said yes. When the lawyer came to me, he was an older African man, I don't think he was South African.

'Are you pleading guilty or not?' he asked.

'Guilty,' I said, firmly.

He looked shocked. 'Are you sure? They might sentence you to twenty-five years, you know!'

'I am sure,' I said.

'You are the first person who has been so sure to plead guilty,' he said, with a surprised expression on his face.

'It is because I am a Christian now. I cannot lie,' I said.

He left me and I just closed my eyes, continuing to pray and trust God.

At about 2 p.m. I was called to court. I stood in front of the judge, a coloured man in his fifties. There was a detective and an interpreter with me as they read out my charge – drug-trafficking. It was recorded that I had smuggled fifty-six bullets of cocaine.

'Mr Pani, do you understand the allegations against you?' asked the judge.

'Yes,' I replied.

'So what will you plead in this matter?'

'Guilty, Your Honour,' I said.

He nodded his head, and then I was taken back down to the cell in court to await sentencing. Fifteen minutes later I was called back and the judge addressed me again.

He said, 'Mr Pani, you are a danger to your country. Are you aware that in South Africa the crime rate is increasing rapidly, because of drugs? Because of you people will have lost their lives. You are South African, what are you doing bringing drugs into your own country?'

I was so ashamed as I knew he was speaking the truth; I nodded at all he said, hoping he could see I was genuinely remorseful.

'You *should* be sentenced to twenty-five years,' he went on. 'But as you have shown remorse, and have not wasted the resources of the state by pleading not guilty, I sentence you to ten years, five years of which will be spent in prison and five years on probation. You may now go.'

I was escorted back to the court cell and, as I waited to be taken back to prison, I started praising God and worshipping him. I sang my favourite song from Sabelo's church – 'Alpha and Omega'. It speaks about God being the beginning and the end, and worthy of all our praise. As I was singing, I felt the Holy Spirit saying, 'Now you have learnt to worship God not for what he can give you, but for who he is.' It felt a very significant moment; God was showing me how important obedience is to him.

'Brother, you look happy – are you free?' asked another prisoner in the cell; he was a young guy who had been arrested for stealing from a shop.

'No, I am going back to prison.'

'Why are you singing then?' he asked.

I sat down next to him and shared my story, how God had forgiven me and given me hope. I explained that he is the only way to be saved.

'Listen, stop shop-lifting,' I said. 'I am going to prison for ten years, but you are young. If you get off, go home, listen to your parents, stay in school. You have a chance at life.'

'I hear you, *groot mann*,' he said, meaning 'big man' in Afrikaans, a term of respect.

We arrived back at Modderbee at about 5 p.m., just as it had started to rain. I had been in relative safety in C-section, but now I was going into the real prison, and I had heard bad stories of molestation and drug-taking. 'Lord, please help me!' I prayed.

16

Being Discipled

The other prisoners I had gone to court with returned to C-section. They had all pleaded not guilty, so were back in the position of awaiting trial.

As I was now sentenced, I had to wear prison clothes. I was taken to a room to remove what I was wearing, even my underwear. In return, I was handed my uniform – the standard orange top and trousers with 'Correctional Services' printed all over, underpants, a blanket and shoes. They didn't give me socks, and I could not keep my old ones, so I would have to find a way of getting some later.

I had my outside clothes in a bundle, and gave them to a homeless guy I had spoken to before court, as he was still there when I got back. What he had was dirty and ragged and I knew he was going to need the clothes more than I was.

At this point I had accepted my fate and was trying to prepare my mind for what was to come. Five years of incarceration. I could not run away from this, I had to face it, and I told myself to toughen up. I decided I would use my time to change my life and live for God. I made the decision not to join a gang, even though I knew that it would be very dangerous for me not to be under a gang's protection, but I had to trust in God.

After I was given my prison uniform, I was handed a card with my prison number, my name and my sentence on. I had to have that with me at all times.

I was then taken out of reception through to 'Block 4' where I would stay for a few months until transitioning to another section in the prison. There were four 'transition blocks' where prisoners would go first. Block 4 had a smaller reception area, and then ten cells with bunks in each, so two prisoners per cell.

'Welcome! This is your new home, get used to it,' said the warden as he explained the rules of the prison. I stood at the door of my 'new home'. It had a bunk bed, a small window high up on the wall opposite the door, and a toilet attached to the far wall. There was a faint smell of sewage in the room.

I nodded to the man sitting on the bottom bunk. He looked in his forties.

'Welcome, brother. I am Thandile,' he said, standing up and greeting me in Zulu.

He showed me my bed and where I could put my stuff. I had a bucket with my toiletries, a towel and my Bible: all my worldly possessions.

'I am a follower of Jesus, are you?' he asked.

'Yes, I just got saved a few months ago.'

'Praise the Lord!' he said, his eyes shining.

I told him the story of going to Sabelo's church and receiving forgiveness for the first time.

'So, brother! We can pray and study the word of God together,' he said, and I wondered at the kindness of God to place me in a cell with a Christian brother who could teach and disciple me.

Thandile told me his story. He was from the Tswana tribe and even though he knew the Lord, and had felt called to be a pastor, he tried to run away from the calling, and gone into IT. The cares and busy-ness of the world had taken him away from God. He had been accused of rape, but was innocent. It was the trauma of being falsely accused that had driven him back to seeking Jesus again.

As we got to know each other, I told Thandile about my girlfriend in Cape Town. I hadn't spoken to her but now I knew my sentence, I had to give her a call. I was nervous to speak to her, I had missed her and thought about her a lot. I stood in line at the communal phone on the first Saturday in Block 4 and, when I got through to her, she was understandably very angry with me.

'How can you do this to me and your mother? You are so selfish. Now you are there and we won't see each other for years,' she shouted down the phone.

I didn't know what to say. I wanted to ask if she would wait for me but I knew I was asking a lot, and that I had not treated her as she deserved.

'You don't expect me to wait for you, do you?' she asked, before I could bring it up.

'No, I won't do that,' I said, sheepishly.

I didn't know what was going to happen with our relationship, but I was still disappointed. I had expected her to wait. I thought we both loved each other. We talked for a while longer, but there was not much more to say. I felt heavy as I walked back to my cell. Thandile was waiting for me.

'How was it?' he asked.

'Not good.'

Thandile shook his head. 'No, my brother. If the Lord wants you to be back with her, he will make it happen, but you need to focus on God now. Let her go.'

I knew he was right, but I would need God to do a work in my heart to truly let go.

Our first morning, Thandile and I prayed, and then opened the Bible together. Thandile sat on the bottom bunk, and I perched on an upturned bucket.

'This is a spiritual book. Read it slowly, with your heart,' he said.

'I am only starting to learn to read,' I said, embarrassed.

'Don't worry, your reading will improve,' he encouraged.

When we were locked in for the night, I flicked through a copy of *People* magazine which was available to the prisoners. Thandile pulled me up on it straight away.

'Stop reading this material. It will not profit you, it will only disturb your spirit and you will be defiled.'

Our routine in Block 4 was similar to that in C-section. Lights went on at 5 a.m., and at 6 a.m. the cell doors were opened so we could present ourselves to be counted. All the inmates squatted outside their cells as the wardens walked past and asked if there were any complaints from the night before. If not, we returned to our cells until breakfast at 8 a.m. Every day we ate porridge, an apple and a mug of tea. We were then free to walk around until 3 p.m. when we were locked in again for the night.

I knew Thandile was right, at that time I just needed to feed myself with the word of God. Thandile and I prayed together every day, and he taught me the importance of fasting. He said it is not about trying to make God do something for you; instead, fasting benefits you in that it helps you be more sensitive to him. Fasting is for spiritual growth.

We fasted each week, sometimes for three days at a time. When we were fasting we would still pick up our breakfast, but instead of eating or saving it, we gave it to those who needed more. Thandile explained this is what we are commanded to do in Isaiah 58:6–7:

> Is not this the kind of fasting I have chosen:
> to loose the chains of injustice
> > and untie the cords of the yoke,
> to set the oppressed
> > free and break every yoke?
> Is it not to share your food with the hungry?

Even when we were not fasting, we were often hungry in prison. There was no comfort given from food as the portions were very small. If you complained, the server would laugh. 'This is not your mother's house, don't expect any extras here,' they'd say.

After about four days on Block 4, Thandile said we must invite the other prisoners to a prayer meeting; I agreed, and was happy to follow his lead. We went from cell to cell, greeting the prisoners. In our culture it is important to greet people. I would open with:

'*Molo, kunjani?*' (Hello, how are you?)

The person would respond with, '*ndiphilile*' (I am fine) and then ask how I was.

We would greet even before fighting with someone, it is so part of life. After greeting my fellow prisoners, I said: 'Brothers, we are having a prayer meeting at 9 a.m., please come and pray with us.'

Most of them seemed disinterested, but some agreed they would come. When we got back to our cell, Thandile told me I must lead the meeting.

'I cannot do that!' I said. First, I was shy, and not confident in speaking, *and* I had only just become a Christian.

But he was firm: 'Don't worry, we will go through the Bible and I will show you what you can share.'

I had little choice but to agree. We sat down together and he opened the Scriptures with me.

Thandile showed me Hebrews 4:16: 'Let us then approach God's throne of grace with confidence, so that we may receive mercy and find grace to help us in our time of need.' He explained that every time I pray, I am approaching God's throne, and I should try and imagine it in my mind. I am then asking for his mercy and grace.

Three other verses he taught me were Hosea 14:2:

Take words with you
    and return to the LORD.
Say to him:
    'Forgive all our sins
and receive us graciously,
    that we may offer the fruit of our lips.'

And 1 John 1:9: 'If we confess our sins, he is faithful and just and will forgive us our sins and purify us from all unrighteousness.' And finally, from 1 Timothy 2:8: 'Therefore I want the men everywhere to pray, lifting up holy hands without anger or disputing.'

He taught me the importance of praying for people in leadership, because Proverbs 29:2 says:

When the righteous thrive, the people rejoice:
    when the wicked rule, the people groan.

And then 2 Chronicles 7:14: 'If my people, who are called by my name, will humble themselves and pray and seek my face and turn from their wicked ways, then I will hear from heaven and I will forgive their sin and heal their land.'

Thandile explained about praying for South Africa. We needed to focus on praying for the leadership and land, so we can be ruled by righteousness. I soaked it all in, the word of God was life to me.

However, the next day I was very nervous. At 9 a.m. it was only Thandile and two other prisoners with me. I started with a welcome: 'I greet you all in the name of the Lord Jesus Christ. We are conducting this meeting as God commands us to pray, and I will lead you in some Scriptures.'

I fumbled with my Gideon Bible in my hand, and the notes I had written down. Reading with my head down, I went through the verses Thandile had shared with me, and when I was finished, we started to pray. We stood in a circle and all started praying out loud. We declared Scripture and petitioned God loudly. Two hours later we were finished. I had led my first prayer meeting and got through it.

'Well done,' Thandile said. 'You can lead tomorrow as well.'

I gulped, but I didn't refuse. I wanted to grow in God and let him use me. Thandile taught me about being an intercessor and standing in the gap for others. We would pray every morning from 9 a.m. until midday. Sometimes it was only one or two prisoners who joined, but at other times we had over fifteen inmates praying with us. As we prayed, we saw answers, but also we experienced persecution. Inmates complained that we were making too much noise. Thandile said we were only following Scripture. Acts 4:24 says: 'When they heard this, they raised their voices together in prayer to God.' If that is what the early church did, then we would too. It goes on to say in verse 31: 'After they prayed, the place where they were meeting was shaken. And they were all filled with the Holy Spirit and spoke the word of God boldly.' We were praying the same thing – that God would shake us and Modderbee prison. Eventually one of the wardens, who was also a pastor on the outside, found us a vacant cell away from the others to pray in.

Thandile would pray in tongues a lot, and sometimes sing in tongues. I asked him how I could pray in tongues too.

'My brother, first read 1 Corinthians 14,' he said.

I turned to the chapter in my Gideon New Testament, and read verse 1: 'Follow the way of love and eagerly desire gifts of the Spirit' and then verse 4: 'Anyone who speaks in a tongue edifies themselves.'

'If you desire the gift, God is faithful and will give it to you, but don't try to imitate another brother's language – God will give you your own tongue,' Thandile said.

I asked God for the gift and read 1 Corinthians over and over to fully understand it.

The following Sunday we were invited to a church service in Block 3, which was an unusual occurrence. A pastor from the outside and his friend were going to lead a service for us. There were about twenty prisoners in chairs along the corridor. The pastor preached and then prayed for us to be filled with the Holy Spirit. As he prayed, I started speaking in tongues. I was so excited that I didn't want to stop! What began as a few words grew to a larger vocabulary. I prayed in tongues to minister to myself and build up my spirit.

After a few weeks, many of the prisoners in Block 4 came to our morning prayer time, even prison officers. There was a revival breaking out as prisoners repented and gave their lives to the Lord. Thandile was prophetic, and God showed him things that were going on in the prison, so we could pray about it. Often it was exposing things that were not good.

One of the original prisoners who had joined our prayer time was a man called Ntsikelelo. He prayed with us each day, but he struggled to fully surrender. He was a few years older than me and in prison for being involved in a house invasion. He didn't come to faith, as he struggled with letting go of ancestry worship, but he was a good guy and became like a brother to me. It was through Ntsikelelo that I finally got some socks. His mother would visit him, so I got Mama to send her money and she brought the socks with her for Ntsikelelo to pass on to me.

There was one Xhosa brother, Siziwe, who was not interested in the gospel at all. He was in prison because he had fought with someone when drunk and killed them accidentally. Every day I shared my faith with him, and he would sneer at my words. 'Ah, no. Jesus is for white people. You are Xhosa and now you are forsaking our traditions. Shame on you,' he would say, shaking his head.

After a month I had to move on from Block 4. The officials decide where you go, and the options were D-, F-, J- and K-sections. J-section was for those focused on finishing school and getting their matric (exams like A levels). K-section was for those who wanted to go to school and work. There was also D-section for the workers – inmates who were working – cleaning, carpentry, woodwork and upholstery. I didn't know much about F-section. There was one more section – 'I' for the 'lifers'. It had much higher security, and you would never choose to go there.

I was moved to K; Ntsikelelo was also transferring there so I would have a friend. I was so sad to leave Thandile as he was staying in Block 4. He had become like a spiritual father to me. When it was time to go, I collected my things, and thanked him. He gave me a hug and told me to keep on preaching and to never stop praying.

'I have a word for you from Isaiah 40:29–31,' he said. '"He gives strength to the weary and increases the power of the weak. Even youths grow tired and weary, and young men stumble and fall, but those who hope in the LORD will renew their strength. They will soar on wings like eagles; they will run and not grow weary, they will walk and not be faint." Brother Shepherd, your journey with God is a long journey, you will face difficulties, but you must trust in the Lord, and he will help you soar.'

I thanked him and hugged him back. He had taught me so much in such a short time.

I was feeling trepidatious going to K-section. I was taken to my new cell, sharing with forty-one other prisoners. This time we had bunk beds instead of mattresses on the floor. I was put on the top bunk, above a Zulu guy called Sipho. He had TB so wasn't well, but as soon as he saw me open my Bible he hated me and spent every moment he could persecuting me.

'You know what, you are only reading this Bible because you are in prison. When you leave you will forget all about it. You are a fraud,' he would sneer.

Sipho tested me, and I had to practise forgiveness, patience and tolerance again and again. Every morning as we stood to be counted, I would greet him, saying, '*Molo*, brother Sipho.' He never responded, everything about me made him angry.

I was thankful Ntsikelelo was with me; we would eat together and pray when we could.

The cell was on two floors, so I made myself a prayer room on the top floor away from all the others. In K-section, people would be smoking drugs in the corridors. Many of the prisoners were involved in perverted things and molested each other, some were attacked and robbed, but I was safe throughout my time in the section. I was called *Umfundisi*, which means pastor or teacher, so I found respect.

It was in K-section that I enrolled in a theological course through Team Work Bible College. Pastor Clinton had a church in Benoni, but was connected to the Team Work Bible College in Durban. He was a coloured guy in his forties and he came every Wednesday to lead a Bible study with us. As I still only had the Gideon New Testament, Pastor Clinton gave me my own, brown-leather, full Bible. He inscribed it with the words: 'To Shepherd, this book will keep you from sin, and sin will keep you from this book.' Those words had a big impact on me.

Now I was in the prison and not the remand cell, I could have visitors. Once a year, every September, there was a 'Family Day'. It was too far for my family to visit from Cape Town, but Ntsikelelo's family came to see me. My mother sent them money to bring me toiletries, such as soap, deodorant and razors. We were only allowed the most basic, yellow-plastic razors to shave in prison.

After six weeks in K-section, I heard about a course being led by Maranatha Community Church called 'Walking in Victory'. It was a week-long course and open to all prisoners. I signed up and it was there I met a man called Uncle William, a pastor from Egypt. He was a short man, in his sixties, and very kind. During the course we all had lunch together, and one day he sat next to me. He asked about my walk with God.

'What do you want to do when you are out of prison?' he asked.

I told him I wanted to finish school, and then study theology to be a pastor.

'Why don't you simply transfer to F-section?' he asked. 'You can get training in theology there.'

He explained the Christ the Only Hope section was run by Maranatha Community Church. 'It started from a trip that Pastor André took in 2006 with the head of Modderbee Correctional Centre, and the then chaplain. They went to Argentina to witness a Christian programme run in their prisons. A local pastor became a warden inside Olmos Prison in Argentina, and he saw God change the lives of the prisoners, so much so that the authorities offered him his own prison to run as a Christian evangelical institution. He called it Christ the Only Hope Prison, and they were able to bring down re-offending from 55 per cent to 5 per cent. Pastor André was given permission to come to try and run something similar in Modderbee.'

It sounded just what I needed. I applied to the officials in K-section, and they sent my application to the chaplaincy for approval. After two months in K-section I was moved once again to my final home in Modderbee prison, F-section.

17

F-section

On 18 August 2013 I was transferred over to F-section. It had been raining the day before, but on the morning I moved in the sun was shining. It was a Sunday, and mid-winter in Benoni. Even though it was cold, it was dry and not rainy like winter in Cape Town. As the metal doors were unlocked to enter F-section, the atmosphere immediately felt different. The first thing I saw was a large board with the words: 'Christ the Only Hope Centre'.

My bag was checked, to make sure I had nothing illegal on me such as a phone, and then the officer walked me to a cell.

'This is Cell 1, your new home. Come and meet the elder.'

We walked towards a huge Afrikaner standing by a bunk. He looked like Arnold Schwarzenegger with his muscled arms bulging out of his orange prison shirt.

'Kaiser, this is Shepherd Pani, you can tell him the house rules!' the officer said and then left.

'Welcome, *boet*, glad you are with us,' he said shaking my hand warmly. He introduced himself as Hendrik Hein Kaiser. I would have been intimidated by him normally, but his friendliness put me at ease.

'OK, house rules – first, are you a Christian?'

I told him how I had recently become a believer and had given my life to Christ at Sabelo's church.

'That is lekker news, brother, you will be happy here. F-section has nine cells, each with forty people. Not everyone is a Christian so, if you want to stay in Cell 1 or 9, you have to show a true faith commitment. Cell 1 and Cell 9 have a leadership team of twelve people, like the disciples, who are appointed as elders. To qualify to stay in Cell 1 or 9, you have to sign a code of conduct, and for Cell 1 you have to commit to pray for an hour a day. Can you do that?'

I nodded. 'Yes, I would be very happy to do that. I have been praying for three hours a day in the other section already.' I said.

'That is good to hear, brother.'

Hendrik took me to a bunk at the end of the room. I was in the top bed as I was a newcomer. I would have to wait until someone moved out before I could grab a space on a lower bunk. As I was last in, it might take a while.

I saw that in the cell they had pushed the bunks closer together, to make a space at the end of the room. The area had a map of the world and some Bible verses written on paper on the wall; there was also a prisoner on his knees praying.

'Come and see,' Hendrik said. 'This is our "prayer room" or "boiler room". We are praying 24/7 for South Africa and the world here.' I was so thankful to be in this cell with like-minded believers. I knew I would grow here.

We left the cell, and Hendrik took me down the corridor. I saw groups of prisoners doing Bible studies together; this was different from any other section in the prison.

In Modderbee there was a ratio of approximately 85 per cent black prisoners, and 15 per cent white, coloured and Indian. However, in F-section we had about thirty white people, and six in Cell 1. I learnt that many of my white brothers had a background of faith, and in prison they were returning to the faith of their youth. Racism was not an issue as we are all equal behind bars. We used the same toilets, ate the same food, and wore the same uniform. The prison wardens did not show partiality to colour. Everyone was treated as a prisoner, because that was what we were.

Hendrik explained that on Tuesday, Wednesday and Friday pastors would visit for teaching, counselling and Bible study. I was excited about the opportunity.

'Why are you here?' I asked Hendrik as we walked around the section.

'I'm from Table View in the northern suburbs of Cape Town . . .'

'I am also from Cape Town, I know Table View,' I interrupted.

'Lucky you,' he smiled. 'It's a beautiful place, but I had a tough upbringing.'

He told me how he left school early and worked as a bouncer in Table View's nightclubs. From there he got involved in people-smuggling and drug-trafficking.

'When I was a young man I was very racist, I hated black people and I had so much anger in me. In my twenties I was eventually caught on drug-trafficking offences, and sentenced to twenty-five years in prison. In my first years in prison, I would beat anyone who annoyed me. I would attack prisoners and prison guards. Eventually I was put in solitary confinement, I was a danger to everyone. Being alone broke me. I'd been arrogant and tough, and thought no one could defeat me, but solitary humbled me.'

Hendrik's eyes had teared up as he told his story. He said someone gave him a Bible, and he started reading it.

'I had an encounter with God in solitary, Jesus came into my cell and spoke to me. He told me to follow him. I felt such love and acceptance from him, and gave him my life. Shepherd, Jesus has changed me from the inside out, I am a different man. God taught me about forgiveness, and dealt with my attitude to black people. Now I love everybody!'

We both laughed, but I could see it was true in the way he talked to me, and communicated with other prisoners.

As I closed my eyes to sleep the first night in Cell 1, I breathed a prayer of thanks to God. I knew that F-section was the right place for me, and that he had made a way to get me there.

The next day felt very similar to mornings on the other blocks. Lights were turned on at 5 a.m., but in Cell 1 we had to get up and make our beds. Every bunk had a small window next to it which we opened to let in fresh air. Once everything was neat and tidy and we were dressed, we could then lie back down on our beds, until cell devotions. Every morning at 5.45 a.m. in Cells 1 and 9 a bell would ring. It was a fifteen-minute warning before devotions at 6 a.m. We had a fifteen-minute service, and it wasn't long before I had a slot every week to bring a word of the day.

Cell 1 is where my faith journey really began. As the days and weeks went by, I felt I was growing in my walk with Christ. Because I had been changed by the love of Jesus, I was compelled to share my faith with others. I would speak to my fellow inmates about Jesus, especially those who had not yet come to faith. Ntsikelelo followed me to F-section, but he stayed in Cell 5. We would still eat together and hang out, but I was focused on learning, so I spent much of my time reading the Bible and other books.

There was another prisoner I befriended from Cell 5, a white guy from Johannesburg called Alex. He was tall with slicked-back black hair. The way he held himself, I could tell he had been successful outside. He was in for three years, convicted of fraud. He was a farmer, and used to lend me his safari and business magazines, and I would share Christ with him. He was an atheist, so told me all about his ideologies around religion. He never came to faith as far as I know, but we became good friends.

I saw how the other guys worked out, and I decided to join them. Every day from 12 noon to 1 p.m. I lifted weights at the gym and then, in the morning and evening, when we were locked back in the cell, I did push-ups. I knew it was important to stay physically fit and healthy, and have some discipline in my life.

There was a TV in Cell 1, but we would only watch news or sport – nothing explicit or violent. On Tuesdays and Wednesdays, Christian DVDs were played. We were the only cell in the whole prison with a DVD-player, which had been donated by Maranatha Community Church. Worship and preaching would be going on in the background, everything from *Focus on the Family* to Louis Giglio to Angus Buchan. Angus was a pastor and farmer from Bloemfontein. I particularly enjoyed his testimony told in the film, *Faith Like Potatoes*. I loved his faith; he prayed for rain like Elijah in 1 Kings 18, and rain came. Angus Buchan was not an educated man, but God used him mightily, and he loved everyone.

Prison became a school for me. I had failed at high school, but by God's grace he had placed me in an institution where

I could learn. We used to called prison the 'school of life' but for me it was also a place of my literal education.

I signed up to do a four-year theological course, through Maranatha Community Church in Kempton Park but, when it started, I almost didn't enrol because of my limiting thinking. I was scared I would not succeed or do well, as I had dropped out of school. However, with the encouragement of Uncle William, I enrolled, and I ended up doing the four-year course in two years. It was designed for people who are working so, as we had more time in prison, we were able to take on more modules. As I studied, my reading and writing improved and I developed an aptitude for learning. I did well and my marks were always the top. As it was Bible-related I often knew the answers, because by this time I was getting to know the Scriptures well from my daily reading and studying. I was also reading other sources and books to support my study.

For my theological diploma there were thirty-seven modules in total. When I was able to 'upgrade' to a bottom bunk in Cell 1, I turned a bucket upside down to make a chair, and use my bed as a desk. As I studied there were moments of feeling, 'Wow, this is so beautiful.' I could feel my mind being renewed, and my thinking changing.

I had made another friend, an Indian brother from Durban named Keegan. He was in for robbery, but had also become a Christian while doing the 'Walking in Victory' course. Keegan was being mentored by Hendrik, who we now all called 'Big Guy', and Keegan would bring Hendrik's food to him as he had a food allergy. We would chat when Keegan came to the cell.

'Shepido!' he would call me, and I in turn called him, 'Keego!'

Keegan and I became covenant brothers – like Jonathan and David in the Bible. We would spend time in the evenings talking about what we were learning, or what God had shown us in his word. Some people were surprised at me not sticking to the other Xhosa men to be friends with, but I had always felt a lack in partiality when it came to people's background or colour.

Every Sunday we had church, run by Pastor André Roodt and the twelve inmate leaders. We had a pastor who came in from outside, a colleague of Pastor André. He was a Malawian called Ezekiel Mpocela, and had an office assigned to him. Keegan ran the administration for Pastor Ezekiel in his office, and we would often meet and pray for people or counsel them there.

Pastor Ezekiel was available from Monday to Friday for prayer and counselling with inmates. There were tea-making facilities in his office, and we made sure it was always clean and tidy. Pastor André was the overseer of Christ the Only Hope Centre, but it was we prisoners who led most of the meetings. I joined the worship team as a backing singer. We had drums, mikes and a full sound system. Every Sunday, visitors came from outside to experience our prison church. Sometimes they would bring a word, but it was mostly we inmates who preached and gave testimonies. The Holy Spirit moved powerfully in our church meetings.

To deal with conflict in F-section there was a 'Disciplinary Committee'. Disputes were taken to the prayer 'boiler room' in Cell 1. There was a structured and organized process for wrongs to be made right. In F-section, inmates are focusing on church and rehabilitation of other inmates in the prison.

We were to be trained to take part in counselling and restorative justice, helping to reconcile relationships with prisoners and their victims and communities.

You can always find out information in prison. News is passed from section to section through the prisoners that work in the kitchens, and deliver the food. I was encouraged one day to get a message from Siziwe, the man who ridiculed my faith in Block 4. He said, 'Brother Shepherd, today I have been born again. Thank you for preaching to me.'

I couldn't believe it, and sent a message back to ask what had happened. He said he had joined Thandile's prayer meetings, and had felt the love of God. Thandile had led him in a prayer of salvation.

Siziwe had to leave Block 4, and he was initially transferred to J, but he contacted me to ask how he could transfer to F. Before moving he was able to come to our church service, and when I saw him again I hardly recognized him – he was glowing. He had shaved off his Afro, and stopped smoking. He had peace in his eyes. We embraced, and I thanked God for what he had done in my brother's life.

I helped Siziwe with his application to F. After a month in J he was transferred, and moved to Cell 9. I looked to him as a seed I had planted, a fruit of my testimony. He had constantly rejected me and the gospel, saying Jesus is not for Xhosa people, but I kept on loving him and now he was a brother in Christ. In Cell 9, Siziwe became a prayer warrior. God restored his marriage and on his release he started a ministry in the Eastern Cape.

People from F-section had special responsibilities to go and preach the gospel in other sections. At first, I was only allowed to carry the projector, DVD and speakers for the pastors who were coming in to run courses. The leaders had to see if I could be trusted, and understood the importance of serving. I would also prepare the hall for Uncle William when he came in.

After just under a year in Christ the Only Hope section, I was appointed one of the twelve leaders, along with Keegan. I had been serving since I arrived, but now I held an official leadership role, and took the position seriously.

At about that time we had a new inmate come to Cell 1. News was quickly filtered through from unofficial channels, and we were told a young guy named David was being sent to F-section, and he was a serial killer. He was being moved from another prison as he had stabbed a warder. The Modderbee officials were sending him to Cell 1, in the hope that we could pray for him.

18

Healing Old Wounds

We were all wondering what this serial killer would look like but, when he arrived, David took us by surprise. He was a short, handsome, coloured guy, about 30 years old. I took some time to talk to him, and he was very polite, a gentle guy. Over the next few days, he would come and talk to me when we were locked in for the night. He said he had family in Cape Town, and we shared stories and I gave him some Scriptures to think about.

He told me that he used to work in a mortuary. He had been approached by traditional healers who asked him to sell them parts of the dead bodies for their medicine. He agreed, but was eventually found out and lost his job. That is when he turned into a killer. He needed money so he murdered people so he could continue to sell the body parts. As I talked to him, I felt God gave me a Scripture, Romans 12:21: 'Do not be overcome by evil, but overcome evil with good.' I understood that you could not conduct deliverance without love. If you have any anger or strife or unforgiveness in your heart, you cannot wage war against the enemy.

David had only been with us for a week when I was woken up in the middle of the night by the sound of shouting. I opened my eyes and saw a few of the prisoners trying to restrain David. They were beating him violently.

'Hey! Stop, don't hurt him!' I shouted.

David was manifesting a demonic spirit that gave him a supernatural strength. He was fighting back and able to move the heavy, steel, bunk beds by himself. It was quite a commotion but eventually Hendrik was able to tie him up with rope that we had in the cell for volley ball.

F-section only had one warden on duty at night; the prisoners were banging on the door shouting, 'Chief!!' until he came. He then had to phone for back-up so it took time to get the prison wardens from other sections to come and deal with David. In the end there were about fifteen officers who came to deal with the situation.

After David was taken away by prison wardens, I found out what had happened from an inmate who had been awake and watched the whole episode.

In the middle of the night David had got up, gone to the bathroom and somehow broken the small window. He took a shard of glass and then went back into the room to the bed of a prisoner called Jonas. Without warning, David attacked Jonas, trying to slash his neck with the glass. Jonas had done nothing to him, and thankfully woke up in time and was able to fight him off. Jonas screamed and shouted, which woke me and others up.

I was heartbroken, as I knew it was the demonic spirit causing David to act as he had done, and we should have dealt with that, instead of using violence. Jesus delivered many people from demonic spirits in the Bible, and he gave us authority to do the same in his name. I felt such regret that I had not prayed with him.

We heard David was placed in a single cell after that, but a few weeks later he did the same thing – broke a window and this time tried to slit his own throat with the glass. David was taken to hospital, and after that he was moved again to another prison so I don't know what happened to him, but I pray David found freedom and deliverance.

In the day-to-day events of prison life, I was also pursuing my own healing from the emotional wounds from my childhood. I took a restorative justice course with a Zulu pastor called Chris Denga. There were about ten of us in the class, and the programme was four weeks long. Pastor Chris spoke about the story of Zacchaeus the tax collector from Luke 19. In verse 8 it says, 'Zacchaeus stood up and said to the Lord, "Look, Lord! Here and now I give half of my possessions to the poor, and if I have cheated anybody out of anything, I will pay back four times the amount."'

Pastor Chris explained the importance of making right our wrongs. As he spoke I had a vision to give back to my community, Samora, when I got out of prison. I had stolen from cars and been drunk and disorderly there. I had not been a role model to younger guys, and now I wanted to be. 'Lord, give me the opportunity to give back and make a difference,' I prayed.

I knew there were people I needed to forgive. Every Saturday I would call my mother, but my conversation changed as I learnt more from the Bible and was convicted by the word of God. After the restorative justice session I asked to speak to Cinci. I had been a rebellious teenager, and cheeky and disrespectful to her. I knew I needed to ask for her forgiveness. I was nervous and even shaking when I asked Mama to pass the phone to my grandmother.

'Cinci, I want to say sorry for all the times when I was rude and disrespectful. Thank you for your kindness to me over the years, and your prayers. I am grateful now for your discipline, please forgive me.'

Cinci was quiet for a moment, and then said, 'I forgive you, Xolani.' Cinci told my mother later she knew at that point I was saved, and was very touched by my words.

Another person I had to forgive was the teacher who shamed me in primary school, the one who laughed at me because I could not read in my Xhosa class. It just so happened that my brother, Vukile, was doing an internship at our old school, and I phoned him when he was on the premises. I asked him to let me speak to the teacher, who was still at the school. He passed over the phone, and I explained who I was, 'I am Pani, the boy that ran out of your class.'

I gave him a few more details and he remembered me, and we had a good conversation. It was very important that I could release forgiveness to this man who had humiliated me and had such a negative impact on my life. I was particularly grateful I had done it when I learnt that he died not long after. I understood that as Jesus had forgiven me, I had to forgive those who had also done me wrong and, in forgiving them, I was released from any bitterness that was hiding in my heart.

Pastor André gave me a book to read called, *Freed by God but Imprisoned by Culture*. It was written by a Xhosa man named Africa Mhlophe. The book was an eye-opener to me, and confirmed what God had already shown me, that even though I love so much of my Xhosa culture, there are some aspects that are not God-honouring, and obeying God must come above culture and tradition. There have been many great Xhosa kings, and people who have changed the course of this nation, such as Nelson Mandela. However, ancestor worship is not God-honouring and in fact traps my people in debt, having to sacrifice animals to appease the ancestors. The book was the beginning of my preparation to meet my family, and speak to them about what I could no longer partake in, now I was a follower of Christ. I would not sacrifice an animal to the ancestors, or visit a sangoma, and I would worship only Jesus Christ.

Pastor André was so helpful, talking through it with me. He often spoke on issues of identity, sinful habits and fatherlessness. One thing he used to say a lot was, 'Insanity is doing the same thing, over and over, and expecting different results.'

I was also counselled by Uncle William and I had an hour with him each week. He was the only man who knew I had learnt to read only a year or so previously. Others just saw me reading the Bible all day, and would never have guessed I had been illiterate. When I confessed my shame, Uncle William always affirmed me. He told me testimonies to encourage me.

One I remember was of a man in Zimbabwe named Pastor Stephen Lungu. His mother was a teenager when he was born, and he ended up alone and living on the streets aged six. He became addicted to smoking glue and marijuana. He had two guns and a knife that he stabbed people with. He became a freedom fighter in Zimbabwe and embraced the Marxist ideology. When he was twenty he saw a gospel tent meeting when he was on his way to blow up a bank. He told his friends to bomb the tent and kill everyone at 7 p.m. However, before they attacked, he decided to go inside for two minutes. A young girl from Soweto was giving her testimony; the more she shared the more Stephen was drawn in by her words. She then invited an evangelist from South Africa to share from the Bible. He spoke from Romans 6:23: 'For the wages of sin is death, but the gift of God is eternal life in Christ Jesus our Lord.' Moved by the power of God, Stephen felt convicted of his sin. He broke down in tears and walked forward, with his weapons, crying for mercy. That became his turning-point. He went to the police, and confessed everything. After eight hours of interrogation, the police said. 'If your Jesus forgives you, then we forgive you too.'

Stephen Lungu could not read or write but was adopted by a missionary, who helped him. This man became pastor of a big church (he sadly died in 2021, aged 79). His story gave me encouragement, that someone with a past worse than my own, who also could not read or write, could be used by God. No one was discounted.

I confessed to Uncle William all the things I had done in the past. We talked through my relationships, and he helped me understand why sex outside of marriage is not God's plan for us. He showed me the importance of the covenant of marriage and how ungodly relationships can bring a soul tie that you need to be freed from.

Learning about soul ties was a revelation to me. When a man and woman come together in sex, according to Genesis 2:24, the couple become 'one flesh' and 'cleave' to one another. This cleaving creates a godly soul tie and establishes a spiritual marriage covenant. But this bond isn't just physical or spiritual; it's emotional and neurological too. God deliberately designed us with neurological bonding mechanisms to help foster healthy loyalty in marriage.

I realized that I had soul ties with many women, especially my ex-girlfriend. At this point I was no longer in contact with her, but my heart was still connected. I studied the books Uncle William gave me on relationships, because in the future

I wanted to get it right. I had come from a life of promiscuity. I had liked hooking up with girls and needed a lot of prayer to be set free from lust and ungodly thinking. My brothers in Cell 1 used to laugh at me, as every time I was asked what my prayer points were, I would say, 'Pray I find a godly wife when I get out.'

In F-section I also worked as a prayer counsellor and I would pray for other inmates. At one point prison warders brought a prisoner from C-section as he was manifesting demons. 'We don't know what to do with him. You Christians need to pray,' said one of the officers, nervously. Apparently the prisoner had been moving the heavy bunk beds without touching them, and the other inmates were terrified.

I took the prisoner, a young coloured guy, to Pastor Ezekiel's officer, where Keegan, a prisoner named Nikano from Cameroon and I prayed for him. We prayed every prayer we knew, but nothing seemed to happen.

'I think we need to go to Thandile,' I said, and the others agreed.

I explained to the officer there was a man of God in Block 4, and he would be able to deal with this man. The officers were obviously desperate, and agreed to take us all over to Block 4.

The prisoner was in handcuffs, and I saw the officers were wary of him; I had only seen him peaceful and quiet, so I was not prepared for what was about to happen. As we got close to Block 4 the man suddenly started screaming and writhing, trying to run in the opposite direction.

'No, no! I can't go there!'

The officers were quick to clamp down on him. 'You are going,' one of them said firmly, pushing him forward.

'There is fire! Fire is coming out of that place.'

There was no fire, but the demons were seeing the fire of God in Block 4. I was holding my Bible, and I touched the man with it as I was trying to push him forward, praying in tongues.

'Ahhh! Get that book away from me! Fire is coming out of it,' he screamed. But it wasn't him screaming, it was the voice of the demon. I realized again the power of the word of God at that point.

Thandile met us, and we went to his prayer room. The man manifested like a cat, jumping on tables on all fours. He then went under one of the tables and wouldn't come out. Thandile commanded him to come out, but he wouldn't budge.

'OK,' Thandile said to us, and the terrified wardens, 'I am going to show you the power of God. I am going to send the fire of God under the table.'

'Fire of God, fall!' he declared, and as he did the demon-possessed man jumped out as if burnt, and then leapt onto the tiny sink in the room, crouching on it like a cat.

His grandmother's voice then came out of him. The voice said she had initiated him into satanism. She said this boy had killed his mother and father-in-law by burning them, and he lived in the tombs. As she spoke through him, he started crying, but his tears were not water, they were blood. I had never seen anything like it, it was as if we had met the demoniac from the Bible in Matthew 8.

Thandile took authority, arresting the spirit and reminding us of 1 John 4:4 (KJV), 'Greater is he that is in you, than he that is in the world.' It took about an hour, but the man was completely delivered and then led in a salvation prayer. When he came back into his right mind he told us he was from Mitchells Plain, but had gone to Jo-burg – he practised astral projection where he could move from one province to another.

'Why couldn't you leave prison, then?' I asked.

'Satan obeys the laws of the country, I cannot leave prison,' he said.

All these experiences were a huge learning curve for me. Putting into practice what I was reading in the Bible, it strengthened my faith and walk with God and made me aware of the spiritual forces that we are fighting in prayer.

God had shown Thandile that the head of the prison was involved in corruption as well as sangoma witchcraft, and he had confronted him. This did not go down well and Thandile was eventually moved to another prison in Pretoria.

In 2015 Hendrik was released from prison. I really missed him, he had raised the bar in F-section and especially Cell 1, calling us to a life of purity and holiness.

At that time Keegan and I were given the chance to go to church outside. We were both trusted enough to be allowed this privilege. The church had provided our cell with some of the teaching DVDs we watched and, as Keegan and I were now leaders, we were invited to go to a church service.

In our orange prison uniform, we were driven to the church in a prison car, and sat in a cordoned-off section. We had to be handcuffed with a chain to our feet, but the officers were nice to us; they said it was just protocol. The pastor greeted us when he got up to speak, and I have never felt such acceptance from a huge auditorium of people. We stayed for lunch, and in the afternoon were driven back to Modderbee. The day was such an encouragement for us. I felt so much love from the people. We had been nervous they would judge us, but once we arrived at the church we were loved and accepted.

I finished my theological training and graduated in 2016, just before I left prison for good. The graduation was a big deal as my mother, Vukile and my old friend Lucky were going to come to it. It was the first time I had seen them since I left for Brazil. When they were ushered into the hall I was very emotional. I just held them and hugged them. I had missed my family so much.

'Wow, little brother, you are taller than me now!' I laughed at Vukile. He had grown, and was already a man, having spent his time in the bush. Lucky was living in Johannesburg at this point so he came too. Ntsikelelo's family had let my mother and Vukile stay with them, which had made it possible for them to come.

The graduation had TV people and photographers from the outside. A well-known pastor, Siphiwe Christopher Mathebula from Hope Restored Ministries, gave a talk. He told us he was the youngest of eight children, and ran away from home aged ten. He lived on the streets for five years. At the age of 15, a woman adopted him from the street. She taught him how to read, and aged 22 he passed his matric.

I was in tears as I listened to him. He was so impressive. He had a mind damaged from drugs, but the power of the Holy Spirit had changed and transformed him. Now Pastor Christopher runs a big church. He spoke on the theme, 'Game Changers'. He said God has entrusted us to transform our communities. I could not forget that message. He was speaking to my heart and I felt vision come alive as I listened. His talk gave me the desire to be a change agent and catalyst in my community when I was released from prison. I wanted to be the voice for holiness in business, to put the gospel first. I wanted to show people that life can be productive when you submit to God, instead of to ancestors. In my culture, the fear is that if you do not honour your ancestors, you will fail and live in poverty. I wanted to teach that with Jesus Christ in your life you *can* be fruitful, not in terms of a prosperity gospel, but living under the blessing of communion with God. It was better to turn to him, than to the occult. Of course we can expect suffering in life, but also we can experience 'the goodness of the LORD in the land of the living' (Ps. 27:13).

19

'Are You Ready to Go Outside?'

At the end of 2016, after I had been in Modderbee for three years, I was informed that I was to be brought in front of the parole board. This was not unusual as I was near the end of my sentence, and when my name was called from the list, I was hopeful. I had not been under any discipline in prison, and my conduct was good. But still, on the day of my hearing, I prayed for grace and mercy. The board had the power to cut my sentence, but also to extend it if they were not happy.

I made sure I looked clean and smart in my prison uniform, with a freshly shaved head; I had continued to shave my head since the stabbing in Samora a few years earlier. I was taken by a guard to a room in the prison with three men sitting at a desk; two were prison officers, and another was an official from the outside. The man sitting in the middle spoke to me in Zulu, after I gave him my prison card.

'Xolani Shepherd Pani?'

'*Yebo, mnumzane*,' I said.

'OK. So, do you think you are ready to go outside?'

'I do,' I replied.

'State your reasons,' said the same man. 'What are you going to do differently? What if you break the law again when you are out?'

I explained I was a changed man, and spoke about my faith in Jesus.

They asked a few more questions, and then I waited in silence while they made their decision. Eventually the middle guy looked up and motioned for me to come forward. He gave me back my prison card. I glanced at it, and saw it had a new release date on it – 7 May 2017, a year earlier than when I was supposed to finish my sentence. I smiled and thanked them.

I walked out of the room jubilantly and went straight to tell Keegan the good news.

'Shepido! God is good!' he said. He only had another year, so would be out soon too.

The next morning it was my turn to lead devotions in the cell. I gave the word, and then let my brothers know that I would be out sooner than I had thought. They all clapped and cheered, and then spent time praying for me.

I only had six months left in prison, so I needed to make it count. I had been asking God what my calling was. I knew I felt passionate whenever we talked about community transformation. I was inspired by the Apostle Paul and the early church, and I got excited with the idea of helping the poor and under-privileged communities. I didn't want to be a pastor specifically, but a leader and role model for young men. I didn't want to just tell people to believe, I wanted to have a way to help them in life too. I started thinking about maybe opening a restaurant, probably because of my previous experience at Kauai – it was what I knew.

A month or so later, in early 2017, I was going to one of the other sections to preach one Saturday. Sometimes a section would be shut down because there had been fighting, or illegal phones had been found. If so, we couldn't go in. Usually it was allowed, and week by week a group of Christian inmates from F-section would set up our speaker and mikes when the men were walking around in the free time. We would start our service by praying over the section and then one of us would preach. I realized after studying theology that I was not a preacher, I was more of a teacher. Preachers share the gospel and the message of the cross, they are evangelists. Teachers expand on the word of God, and I loved to expound on the Scriptures, line upon line, precept upon precept. Explaining the Scriptures made me come alive and God gave me the grace to teach.

Before we were taken to lead a service in another section, we had to meet in the chaplain's office. This time, as I arrived, I saw Sabelo walking away down the corridor. It was the first time I had seen him since leaving C-section almost four years previously. I called out his name, and started running after him. He stopped and turned around, waiting for me. I was not sure he even recognized me.

'Man of God,' I said, out of breath. 'My name is Shepherd, I wanted to tell you my life has never been the same since coming to faith at your church service.'

Yoh, I could tell he was so blessed by hearing this.

I explained to him what had happened to me, and the impact it had on my life.

'Thank you for telling me, my brother,' Sabelo said with tears in his eyes.

We could not stay talking for long but I was glad I was able to let him know the impact his faithfulness had had on me.

The day of my release from Modderbee Correctional Service came. I had to wake up early as I would be travelling to Cape

Town and it was a long drive. At 3.30 a.m. I was taken to reception to change into my outside clothes. As I had given my clothes to the homeless guy four years earlier, Ntsikelelo's mother had brought me some blue jeans, *takkies* and a shirt. I was given my bag with all my old things in – including the CDs that I had with me in Brazil. It was a very weird feeling looking through that bag, it was like a time capsule, belonging to a very different person from who I had become.

I left the prison at about 4 a.m., driven in a Toyota Corolla by two Afrikaner prison guards. It was going to be a fifteen-and-a-half-hour drive from Modderbee to Pollsmoor prison in Cape Town, but I had such favour with the guys. They bought me food and biltong whenever we stopped, and I shared my testimony with them. They were not Christians but one of them said, 'I'd encourage you to follow the ways of God, *boet*, it's the best way to stay out of trouble.'

It felt exciting to be back in my home town. Seeing Table Mountain coming closer and closer on the horizon, I felt emotional, but I was nervous for my next steps, and I didn't want to go back to my old ways. We arrived in Pollsmoor at about 7 p.m. that evening. When we pulled in through the prison gates, I heard someone shouting my name: 'Hey, X! X-man!'

I tried to lean around to see who it was, but I didn't recognize the person. It was a wake-up call that the old me was known in Cape Town.

I was taken into the reception area at Pollsmoor, and immediately felt oppressive darkness. I prayed in tongues under my breath, asking for God's protection. I was taken into a room where I met with a Pollsmoor prison officer. He asked for my prison number and which prison I had been in. He then asked what number gang I belonged to.

'I am not part of a number, I belong to Jesus,' I said.

He looked at me with raised eyebrows, as if I was joking. 'Come on, what number?' he asked.

'I'm serious. I am born again.'

He shook his head and wrote something on a piece of paper. I heard that sometimes the prison officers were initiated in the gangs too, and I didn't know who I could trust.

I was given a one-bed cell to stay in until my papers were processed and I could be officially released. As I lay down, I saw someone had drawn a demonic picture on the wall, of a man trying to hang himself on a mountain, and then people falling down the mountain and a large group of dead people at the bottom. I felt such spiritual unease in the place that I stayed up most of the night praying in tongues. I woke early the next day, and I knew I was going to be let out soon, so I didn't go to breakfast. I didn't want to get into any trouble with other prisoners, and I was also too excited to eat.

At 10 a.m., an officer came to collect me, and I had to wait in reception until a car was ready for me. I got chatting to a young guy, I began to share the gospel with him. It seemed he was really listening and interested in what I was saying. I was called to go, so I said goodbye to him, and shook his hand.

As I was driven out of Pollsmoor's gate, I checked in my pocket, and my R50, the only money I had, was gone. 'Yoh!' I laughed to myself. All my time in Modderbee and I was never robbed, twenty-four hours in Pollsmoor and my money was stolen!

It was a twenty-minute journey to Mitchells Plain Correctional Services. Mama would meet me there, but more paperwork needed to be done first. The officer explained that as I still had five years to finish my sentence, I had to come every week to sign in at the police station. From 8 a.m. to midday I had work duties, mopping the floors and cleaning the cells as part of my community service. The officer in charge of me was a kind man.

'Pani, if you get a job, you can do your signing on Saturday. You have to be home by 5 p.m. each day. We will come and check you are home, and you will only have one warning. If you are not home a second time you will have violated the conditions of parole, and I'll have to send you back to prison.'

This was something I definitely did not want to do. 'I will be home,' I said.

After everything was completed, I was allowed out. Mama was in the waiting-room. She was wearing her straight, black, bob wig with a scarf around her head, a white T-shirt with her cross-body handbag, a long skirt and sandals. She looked just as I remembered her.

'My son! You are so fat!' she said, which in our culture is a compliment, and opened her arms for an embrace.

I laughed, my weight-lifting in prison was showing on my body.

We opened the main door, and I stepped into the sunlight as a relatively free man. My eyes squinted under the sun's rays. After four years in prison, mostly spent inside, it took my eyes a long time to get used to the strength of the sun.

'What do you want to eat, my boy?' Mama asked.

'Fish!' I had missed Cape Town's fish when up in Benoni.

We went to a fast-food restaurant called 'Fish and Chips' in Mitchell's Plain, and I relished every taste of fried snook and chips.

When I was finished, we made our way to Samora. I looked out of the window of the taxi; everything seemed the same, but I was so different. Arriving at home I greeted Cinci, Vukile and my sisters.

'X, you are so big, look at your muscles!' said Pamela.

'You are so white, and so old-looking!' laughed Phumesa. Because I had spent so long out of the sun, my skin had gone a paler shade.

We all sat down together, and I told them my journey. It was very important for me to share my testimony straight away, so they knew I was not the same Xolani, I was now Shepherd.

'Sho, we can tell you are a changed man,' said Phumesa.

I asked if I could pray, and together as a family we bowed our heads; I thanked God for his blessing and protection. Cinci said amen loudly when I had finished.

'What are your plans now, my boy?' Mama asked.

'I will stay here for a month, look for work and then find a place to stay,' I said.

I was adamant I must keep moving forward.

My first Sunday back, I wanted to go to the church where I had gone to the crusade all those years before. The church had now moved to Woodstock; I got to the right building after the service started. There were about a thousand people all worshipping in an industrial-type building on Station Road. When the worship ended, I saw the preacher was the same pastor who had preached for the crusade meeting, Pastor Elijah. At the end of the sermon I saw Pastor John who had taught the Bible study I attended before my second trip to Brazil, and went to greet him, and tell him what had happened to me. He was so encouraged to hear my story and prayed for me.

That evening I went home on a high, excited about my next steps. My sister, Pamela, was at Cinci's house when I arrived, and I enthusiastically told her about church.

'I want to hear more, but I have to pick up Indiphile – why don't you walk with me to the day care and you can tell me more?' she suggested.

'Of course,' I said, and we made our way down the road to pick up her daughter.

'Remember Zuzeka? The day care is run by her mother. They are a group of Christians like you who live there – you should meet them,' Pamela said.

Zuzeka was a few years younger than me, but I had known her since we were children visiting Cinci in Samora in the holidays or at the weekends. I knew she had been into partying like me, so it was news that she was now a Christian.

When we arrived, Zuzeka was there, and Pamela introduced us properly. 'This is my brother, back from prison.'

'I remember you,' Zuzeka smiled. She was very beautiful, and I found myself smiling back at her.

'He is a Christian, like you,' Pamela added.

'Oh,' Zuzeka said with another smile. 'We have a prayer group you can join if you want.'

'I'd like that,' I said, still grinning.

Zuzeka was part of the Ark of Glory church too. They had a small group with two other girls and a guy. I went along that evening, excited to get to know Zuzeka more.

For the next week I was busy working. Mama had got me temporary employment working in the garden of her boss in Claremont. This gave me money for transport which I was grateful for.

After the service the following week, my friend Lindile handed me a flyer. It was from an organization called the Message Trust, based in Woodstock. They were offering help for ex-offenders to get jobs. I am a man of action, and I made a decision then and there to visit the Message the next day. I had learnt that I needed to take every opportunity handed to me, and let God do the rest.

The next morning I woke up feeling tired. It was cold and raining, and I was warm in bed. I was planning to go to the Message, but I told myself, 'Bro, you need to relax, you need to enjoy sleep.' During all the years in prison I could not enjoy sleep as I had to wake at 5 a.m. every day. Suddenly I realized what was happening. I had been home for two weeks, and this was the only day I was tempted to stay in bed, the day I planned to go to the Message. I realized this was going to be an important part of my next step. I pulled off my covers, got out of bed and got dressed, ready for whatever I was going to find.

20

Divine Appointments

The Message Trust building was easy to find; it was on the main road in Woodstock, and I ran part of the way from the taxi, to try and get out of the rain. It was winter in Cape Town and I needed my beanie to stay warm. I wasn't nervous, even though I knew there was a stigma attached to ex-offenders. The Message flyer had a picture of a prisoner, and said they worked in prisons, so I hoped this would be a place where I would be welcomed.

When I arrived, I was greeted by a Xhosa man who looked a few years older than me.

'Hello, my brother. How can we help you?' he asked.

'My name is Shepherd. I've recently been released from prison and I am looking for work. Can I speak to the manager?' I asked.

'OK, OK, that is great news. Yes, you can,' he said, introducing himself as Steve Sam. 'You have come on a busy day. Everyone is about to go out to do ministry, but take a seat. Let me find someone for you to talk to.'

I sat down at a table, looking around the room. There were a few other guys working at small tables. After a few minutes, another Xhosa guy came into the room with Steve. They walked towards me and I stood up to greet them.

'Welcome to the Message, Shepherd. I am Vuyo Nyabaza,' said the second man, giving me his hand to shake.

Vuyo told me he was in charge of the prison side of the organization. Like Steve and the other guys around me, he was an ex-offender. We sat down and talked, and I told him a bit of my story, how I had given my life to Jesus in prison. I said I wanted to serve my community and help other young men who were in my position.

'Hey, brother, let me take your name and number, and I suggest you come back next Monday for our prayer day, so you can meet everyone,' Vuyo said.

I gave him my details, and then he told me to stick around if I wanted to. I stayed for most of the day. There were a few people remaining and I chatted with them, sharing stories and experiences.

Vuyo said he could drop me off in Samora. He was a pastor, and lived in Gugulethu. I got into his grey Mazda, and we had a good chat in the car. I felt I had found a brother in the Lord. When I got home, I gave a silent prayer of thanks to God. Psalm 37:23–4 says, 'The LORD makes firm the steps of the one who delights in him; though he may stumble, he will not fall.' When I was in prison I had asked God to direct and establish my steps after my release; I could already see him working in my life. After only a day I felt known and understood by the Message guys, and welcomed like a long-lost brother.

For the next week I continued working in the garden of Mama's boss in Claremont, and spent my evenings with Zuzeka's Bible study and prayer group. The following Monday I arrived at 8 a.m. for the Message prayer day. I was welcomed in, and there were around thirty people in a meeting room.

We started with coffee and snacks, and Vuyo introduced me. Everyone was very friendly, and I met some English people who worked for the Message; they explained the trust was founded in the UK in 1988. It felt great to be in a community of believers, like my prison brothers.

The prayer meeting started with worship, then someone preached from the Bible, and that was followed by the centre manager, Mark Slessenger, vision-casting for the year. Then it was time for testimonies. I got up, and stood in front of everyone. This would be the first time I was sharing my testimony outside of prison to people who were not my family. I greeted them, and explained how my life had been changed by Jesus Christ, how I had overcome illiteracy, and now wanted to go and tell young people they have hope in Jesus. I had tried drink, drugs and suicide, and wanted to tell others they are not the answer.

They clapped when I had finished, cheering me on for the transformation Jesus had made. In the break Vuyo came to sit with me.

'We love your heart, and everything you said. We have a programme called "Re-integration" – it's a month long, and we give you a small stipend. Would you like to join?'

I said yes straight away.

That evening I told my new prayer group the good news. I realized I really cared about Zuzeka's reaction. I noticed her humility and love for God. She loved the Bible, and I could see there had been a genuine transformation in her. I took time to get to know her. She was the mother of two girls, Zizo and Zintle. She told me that after the birth of her second daughter in 2013, she was unhappy with the life she was leading, and wanted to pursue God. She came to faith in Jesus at that time.

I knew I had found a rare treasure in Zuzeka, so I didn't want to waste time. In prison, I had prayed again and again for a godly wife, and I believed God was answering my prayers. We spent more time together and, from watching Zuzeka, I saw she was a woman who loved to pray. She loved God and loved people. She was soft and tender, where I was often straight-talking and tough. I knew I needed what she carried.

After only two weeks, I told her I was very interested in her and, when we were walking home from the small group, brought up the subject of developing a relationship with her. She said she felt the same about me.

I knew marrying Zuzeka would make me a father to her daughters, but I was ready for the responsibility. I understood that Joseph was the stepfather of Jesus, and he had embraced his role. Many others in the townships had raised children who were not biologically theirs. My father had done it with my three older siblings, and I knew the love I had for Zuzeka meant I would love her children too. I wanted to be a father figure in the community, and I had to start by being a father figure for the girls.

As I was courting Zuzeka, I was also learning a lot at the Message. I did the month-long Re-integration course, and then was sent on a two-week barista training course at Learn2Earn, so I could get a job working at the Message café in Mowbray. It was then called the Mess Café. As I had worked at Kauai I thought I had an understanding of coffee and the hospitality industry, but what I learned about coffee in the barista course was all new to me. They gave us lessons on the techniques of producing coffee, how it is ground and brewed. I realized making coffee was a scientific process, and I loved learning. We were told the origin story of coffee, that it was discovered by an Ethiopian goat-herder named Kaldi. He herded goats in the ancient coffee forests on the Ethiopian plateau. One day he noticed his goats had extra energy when they ate the beans. He tried them and felt the same, so he took the beans to the monks. One of the monks made a drink with the berries and found that it kept him alert through the long hours of evening prayer, and so 'coffee' was born.

I was interested that coffee was discovered by a shepherd. It was then that I believe God gave me the idea of starting a coffee company, and naming it Malusi ('shepherd' in Xhosa) Coffee. I didn't know how I would do it, but I trusted that if God was in it, he would help me.

After my training I started working at the Mess Café, which was later renamed Gangstar Café. I loved working there as it felt more like ministry than work. We could talk to the customers about the gospel and pray for whoever asked for prayer.

I remember one lady who came in. She was in her fifties, and she asked about the name of the café. I told her many of us had been in gangs or prison but, because of Jesus, we had been redeemed and, as Philippians 2:15 says, we will: 'shine among them like stars in the sky'. She was touched by what I was saying, and would come in for coffee and to hear more about Jesus. One day she brought her son, who was in his early twenties and had been caught up in drugs. He had already been in and out of prison. 'Will you pray for him?' she asked.

'Of course,' I said, and went to sit with her son. We talked a bit and I shared my story. We were able to find him a place in a discipleship house for men, run by the Message. He is now off drugs, recovered and in employment.

I remembered how I used to be at Kauai, too unsure of myself to be at the till. It is true that in Christ we are a new creation (2 Cor. 5:17). I no longer felt the shame of my past. Before prison I was in an identity crisis, but now in Christ I knew my identity. I had confidence that when I spoke, God would speak through me.

21

The Future and Coffee

Zuzeka and I sat together in her room discussing our future. She had her own space in her parents' yard, so we had some privacy. I sat nervously on a chair, while she perched on her bed.

'Zuzu, I want to marry you, but I can't afford the lobola,' I said, referring to the bride price. I held my breath waiting for her response.

She smiled and, encouraged, I went on, 'I want to honour God in our relationship, and keep sex for marriage.'

'Me too,' Zuzeka said, coming closer to take my hand in hers. I was so relieved we were on the same page. I knew if she accepted me with those caveats and in the state I was in, with no money, it was a good sign!

If I had had the money I would have gone with some male relatives to her parents to ask for their daughter's hand in marriage, and agree the bride price. But in my current circumstances, I would have to work for a long time to save enough money. Zuzeka and I decided she would speak to her parents to see if they would let her go ahead and marry me without the lobola being paid up front. I was nervous; they could say no, and then we would have to submit to them.

However, the next day she spoke to her parents, Nosakhele and Themba Futshane. Zuzeka explained she loved me, and that at the moment I could not pay the lobola, and I had no father to pay it for me. Although they didn't really know me, Zuzeka's mother knew my sister Pamela well, from looking after her daughter. She knew my background, but also saw my commitment, and that I was serious and disciplined. This all worked in my favour, and thankfully they agreed we could get married. The bride price was the equivalent of three cows, and I could pay it off as I earned money, bit by bit.

I knew premarital counselling was important from my theological training in prison, and I wanted Zuzeka and I to have a good foundation, so I set out to find a counsellor who we could have some sessions with. When I prayed about it, Pastor Unati Magadla came to my mind. He had been a policeman, was in his late forties, and now ran a gym on Cinci's street in Samora. He had a vision to help the community, and was having a big impact there. My brother Lungile knew him, and I had visited his gym a few times. Pastor Unati studied theology through a church in Strand, run by Pastor Alan Beck. I knew of the church as I had been told about it while still in prison. I would have attended, but it was too far from where I lived.

I contacted Pastor Unati and he and his wife, Ahluma, agreed to meet with us. They were a power couple, doing amazing things for the kingdom of God, and they were perfect role models for us. They too had turned away from Xhosa culture of ancestral worship to honour God and live according to the Bible.

We met with them for four Sunday afternoons after church. Our time with them helped us so much. We learnt about not coming into the marriage with pre-existent expectations; it was a revelation for me. The pastor explained that children and in-laws must not come in between our relationship. The priority in relationships are God first, then spouse, and then children.

Once we had started counselling, I had to find a priest who had a licence to marry people, as our pastors did not. Eventually I found a Catholic priest online. I reached out to him, explaining we wanted to get married soon. He initially asked if we had counselling, and I confirmed we were having it. Then he asked what type of wedding we wanted.

'It is going to be small and intimate, in a home. We will not be booking a hall,' I said.

Zuzeka and I both believed it was unwise to go into debt for one day of our lives. The wedding is about the marriage, and that is what we were focusing on. He seemed pleased with this.

'Every couple I have married where the wedding was not a big affair, they have lasted, but the marriages that have fancy weddings fall apart. You guys will build together, buying all first things together. This marriage will last!' he asserted.

We were encouraged by his words, as we were both still fighting the cultural expectation of a big wedding. Many of our friends and family members were surprised at our choice to get married so quickly, and also to turn away from Xhosa traditions. Usually, when a couple from my culture get married, the wife has to be initiated into the husband's family, to come under the blessing of his ancestors.

If my father had been alive, and we had chosen to follow this tradition, I would have gone with him to Zuzeka's parents. He would have offered them alcohol, and they would have slaughtered a goat. The wife-to-be has to eat a portion of the goat to signify coming under the new ancestors. She then takes her husband's clan name.

We of course did not do this, because as Christians we understood that any form of ancestor worship does not honour God. But breaking away from the social norms, and not following traditional routes, meant people told us we were crazy. Usually when a couple get married there is huge celebration in the community but, with us, there was just silence. No one cheered us on, apart from our new Christian brothers and sisters. Our community didn't think our marriage would last, or they assumed Zuzeka was pregnant, and that was why we were marrying so fast. We felt the pressure from our community, and had to keep turning back to the Lord.

A date was set for 12 November 2017, six months since I had been released from prison. The wedding ceremony was held in Zuzeka's cousin's house in Samora. Only our families and Pastor Unati and his wife came. And it was only Zuzeka and I who dressed up for the occasion. I wore a pale blue suit and white shirt, and Zuzeka wore a traditional dress in pink fabric with flowers on. There were no songs or speeches, but everyone prayed for us, and after the ceremony we had a meal of chicken, rice and salad. I was elated that we had done it, our relationship was now under the covenant blessing of God, and we could move forward together.

We had no money for a honeymoon, so we stayed for three nights in my room at Cinci's house, until we were able to find a room to rent in Samora. We had very little, just a bed, kettle and a bath initially, but bit by bit we saved up for what we needed.

Zuzeka had done a business course with the Christian ministry, Beautiful Gate. Her main income came from being a hair stylist working from home. Sometimes she was also hired to work at a salon in Claremont.

Being married brought a stability to me, and I could feel God's favour and blessing on my life. Choosing marriage and commitment over my old ways of playing around was good for me, and pleasing to God.

I was enjoying working at Gangstar Café and was given more training to be able to train others with Red Band Barista Academy in Port Elizabeth. Three of us with Mark Slessenger went up for the week-long training at the Father's House church, staying all together in an Airbnb in Summerstrand. When we returned, Mark Slessenger came to speak to me and another barista as we were packing up for the day.

'We have been given funding to start another café in the Durbanville area. If you are up for it, we will send one of you to set it up. I'll get back to you with what we decide.'

I had a sense then that it might be me, as my friend had been with Gangstar in Mowbray since the beginning. Sure enough, a week later Mark came to me and asked if I would be willing to go and work on the new café. I wanted time to think about it, and that evening I talked it over with Zuzeka. I realized this was an opportunity to learn the ins and outs of starting a coffee shop. God had placed the desire in my heart to open a business. If I said yes to the challenge, and took note of every detail, I could learn and succeed in the future. I knew I would not be sent alone – Mark Harrison who had been the manager at Gangstar would also be working on the new venue.

The next day I saw Mark Slessenger and told him I would do it.

'Great!' he said, giving me a fist bump. 'Shepherd, this café is your baby. We trust you and believe you are ready for this responsibility.'

We talked through the details and straight away I was given decision-making powers.

'Can you go to the venue, and decide where you think the counter should be, and choose the colours for the interior design and branding?' Mark Slessenger asked.

'No problem,' I replied. It felt good that they were asking for and trusting my opinion. I was jumping in at the deep end, but I had lots of support around me.

Later I worked with Mark Harrison, procuring the suppliers for the cutlery and crockery, the blenders and the toastie machine. I really enjoyed coming up with the roasting recipe for the coffee beans. I had been taught how at my Learn2Earn course and it was great fun to put my training into practice.

We opened in February 2019 in a small shop in the Durbanville Centre mall. I had another barista to work with me, Thembe Xhosi, also an ex-offender. My role was to manage and disciple him. Every morning we prayed together before the store opened, and I shared a short devotion. During the day I would chat with him, counselling as we worked. It wasn't hard as he was a great guy, and we made a good team.

It took two taxis to get from Samora to Durbanville, and I was trying to pass my driver's test and save for a car so I could drive direct from home. Passing my test was proving difficult, as I refused to give a bribe. As a result, I failed the first three tests I took in Mitchell's Plain. The night before my fourth attempt, I woke up at 2 a.m., worried about the test.

'Lord, you know my heart, I don't want to bribe, and anyway I don't have the R3,500 bribe money. I need your help, please help me find favour and pass my test.'

I went back to sleep and with some trepidation went to my test in Philippi the next day. I had decided to go to a new area to see if it would help.

'If you go there, you won't pass if you don't have the bribe money,' said my driving instructor, as the instructors were often recipients of part of the bribe.

'No, don't worry, I will pass,' I said, with more faith than I was feeling.

When I went into the office, my heart sank, I couldn't believe it – there were three traffic cops, two men and one woman. One of the men had overseen my previous test and failed me in Mitchell's Plain. However, before I could panic, the woman stood up.

'Mr Pani, I will take your test. Follow me,' she said.

I silently followed her, and she smiled as I got into the car. She was a Muslim lady and was very kind and respectful. 'Mr Pani, the test is scored based on penalty points, and you can fail if you exceed the allowed maximum, but you are allowed up to eight minor faults,' she explained.

I had never been told that; I thought one wrong thing was a fail, as that had been my previous experience. The test went perfectly, and I passed. I was so relieved. I dropped in on my driving school on the way home to let them know I had got my licence. My instructor looked disappointed – he wouldn't be getting any bribe money from me!

I wanted to get a car, as it would make my life much easier, especially driving to Durbanville. Zukeka decided she was going to join a *stokvel*. This is a type of credit union where a group of people enter into an agreement to contribute a fixed amount of money into a common pool weekly, fortnightly or monthly for a fixed purpose.

'This is how we can save for a car,' she said.

I thought it was a good idea but, before we joined, we were having lunch with some friends. They were from California, and I had become friends with their son at the Message. In August 2019 I was telling them about our plan and, out of the blue, they offered to buy us a vehicle. I was overwhelmed, and told them they didn't have to. They went ahead, and we were able to get a 2006 Chevrolet, which became a massive blessing to our family.

In March 2020 Covid arrived, and with it lockdowns. For a period we could not open the café, and I was stuck at home. It was a time of great anxiety for many South Africans. We knew lots of people in Samora who needed to look for work just to buy enough food for the day. There was extra pressure for us, as we would soon have another mouth to feed.

We had not been trying for a baby, but when Zuzeka told me she was pregnant, I was so excited. After the scan we found out we were expecting a boy. We named him Nkazimo, which means 'glory'. Zuzeka and I both marvelled at the goodness of God, to have taken us from broken and dysfunctional lives to giving us a hope and a future. Our son's name pointed to his goodness to us. Nkazimo was born at Somerset Hospital in Cape Town in June 2020.

Because of Covid, I was not allowed into the delivery room, but thankfully there were no complications. I felt emotional when I eventually was able to hold my first-born son. Cinci had died at home in bed the day before – a life had gone, but now a new life entered the world. I mourned my grandmother, and was grateful our relationship was fully restored before she died.

During that time, I felt God was speaking to me about stepping out and beginning the journey of starting my own business. This felt very scary; I was worried about putting my family in jeopardy. I was feeling the pressure of supporting my wife and son. One morning at home, I cried out to God for encouragement.

'I need a verse, Lord!' I said. Into my head popped Proverbs 24. I read it from The Passion Translation® on my phone. Verse 3 says: 'Wise people are builders – they build families, businesses, communities. And through intelligence and insight their enterprises are established and endure.'

One of the reasons I wanted to start a business was to help the impoverished community in Samora. I had a passion to be part of community development, building hope and teaching the leadership skills that I had learnt in prison to young boys, so they could lead their families in the future and be a positive influence.

I was so excited about the passage that I ran to tell Zuzeka.

'Zuzu, look at this verse! I have never read it before,' I said, putting my phone in front of her face. She squinted, trying to read what I was showing her.

'It says wise people are builders! We have to build!' I explained.

'OK, Shep, OK!' she said, laughing at my excitement.

The verse kept speaking to me over the next few months, I couldn't get away from it, and I knew it meant I was going to have to step out from the security of the Message café. I loved working there, but I believed I had to focus on building, and to do that I needed to make more money. I explained to

Mark Slessinger what I felt; he was sad I was going, but encouraged me to obey what I believed God was saying. Because of Covid, it was hard to meet in person, so I did not have an official leaving event, but I was prayed for, and will be forever grateful for the opportunities and training the Message gave me.

I now had the problem of providing for my family, but thankfully I had a car so I went to work as an Uber driver. Before I left the Message, my friend MK had mentioned the Silulo Foundation, founded by Luvuyo Rani, a man from Khayelitsha. I remembered he was the person who had made my first CV all those years ago. MK explained he had formed the Silulo Foundation to train and empower entrepreneurs, to give back to the communities they are from.

'They might be able to help you,' MK suggested.

'Yes, good idea,' I said, but in reality I was so focused on work and surviving that contacting them went out of my mind.

A few weeks later I picked up an Uber call from Loop Street in town. It was two Xhosa women who wanted a ride to the Waterfront. We made small talk, and I mentioned I was hoping to start a coffee business.

'I work for the Silulo Foundation. We help set up township businesses. You must apply for our course!' one of them said.

There it was again, the Silulo Foundation. This time I took note of it. I dropped the women off at the Waterfront, and a few minutes later my phone pinged. My passenger had sent me the link to register at Silulo. I looked up the ten-week course – the total cost was R5,000, but I could pay R500 (£25) monthly. I read about what they did, giving training in marketing and strategy, teaching on tax law with eighteen steps for successful entrepreneurship leading up to the launching phase. I knew it was what I needed, and I believed God was putting this opportunity in front of me. I registered then and there and started the course in August 2023.

The first thing I learnt was that I should not work *in* my business, but *on* my business. If you get stuck working in your business, you never have time to focus on systems and scaling-up. Also they explained the importance of having a business and a personal bank account, and never mixing the two. Black businesses in South Africa often start without any capital, so it is tempting to spend the profits as soon as they come in.

All this time I was continuing to read the word of God. I was struck by seeing that Abraham was a man who had faith in God. The Bible says, 'Abraham believed God, and it was credited to him as righteousness' (Rom. 4:3). But Abraham was also practical as well as being a man of faith. He had livestock and was shrewd in business. After Jacob married Rachel, he became an entrepreneur to provide for his family, following a dream from God to increase his flocks (Gen. 30 – 31). Boaz had a field and crops; Aquila sewed clothes and had a business to look after the poor, which is what I wanted to do. Even Paul was a tent maker, and in 1 Thessalonians 2:9 he says: 'Surely you remember, brothers and sisters, our toil and hardship; we worked night and day in order not to be a burden to anyone while we preached the gospel of God to you.'

I saw how faithful followers of Jesus were involved in business for the glory of God, and I prayed God would give me the chance to do the same.

During this time I was still going weekly to Nyanga Police Station for my parole stipulations. The day came when I had completed my service; like my prison sentence it had been reduced for good behaviour. I cleaned the cells for the last time, and swept outside the station. It had been a good experience, I had been able to speak to the prisoners about my faith. One had even joined the Job Readiness Course at the Message Trust.

At midday I took my overalls off (it had been dirty work so I hadn't wanted to mess my clothes), and went to say goodbye.

'I'm finished,' I said to my officer.

He looked at me and smiled. 'We mustn't see you here again, neh?'

'You will never see me here again, Chief, I promise you!' I said, and walked out of the station door to my freedom.

Epilogue – 2025

Looking back over my life so far, I am deeply impacted by seeing God's hand of protection over me, before I even knew him. I could easily have died working as a mule, my stomach filled with cocaine bullets. Before that I often took my life in my own hands, drinking to excess and driving under the influence. God spared my life and made a way for me to know him.

After my training with Siluso, I was taken on by Red Band Barista Academy to be their Western Cape Regional Trainer, made possible by my training at Gangstar. It was an amazing opportunity, as it enabled me to have contact with the very people I wanted to employ and disciple. I did my first week-long training in Durbanville for a non-profit organization in January 2024, and then with U-turn, a homeless charity, in March 2024. I am now working with the Chrysalis Youth Development Academy to train the young people to become baristas.

In March 2024 I became a father again. Zuzeka gave birth to another boy, Nqobile (meaning courageous). He was also born in Somerset Hospital, Cape Town, but this time I was able to be in the delivery room and see my son come into the world. I was the first person to hold him, and we have a special bond.

I am now called Tata, not just by my sons but in the community, something that is hard to get used to, as I feel a young man still.

A year after Nqobile was born, I was given a permanent space to serve coffee at the Silulu Business Centre in Milnerton. I applied for grant funding from the Department of Tourism to buy a coffee machine and grinder, and I have been able to employ a former student, who I trained to be the barista. My dream is becoming a reality bit by bit.

These steps are all God's favour, and I believe I will see the fulfilment of my vision – to build a community hub in Samora. My heart is broken to see boys and young men living for alcohol, and seeing it destroy lives. My vision is to create a place for skills development, a coffee shop to train baristas, a place where young men can come off alcohol, and a place of hope and safety. I want to give back to Samora because of what the Lord has done for me. I believe the vision is from God, as it is about others. Men dream for themselves, God's vision is always about blessing others.

I have been constantly inspired by the story of Kaldi, the Ethiopian shepherd who discovered coffee. I am fascinated that he was an ordinary boy, like me, and he discovered something extraordinary that would change the world.

When I look at my life, I see that I am a simple boy from a township, a boy who never thought he would succeed in anything in life. But God . . . ! I discovered the Lord Jesus, and later a love for making coffee. Now I believe God is building my business to change the community and transform the lives of young men who are trapped in hopelessness, drug-taking and violence. There is hope that if God can use a simple boy like me, he can use you. No life is beyond hope or redemption.

There are so many people I want to thank for where I am today:

Pastor Andre, the late pastor William and Pastor Ezekiel for discipling me while I was in prison.

The Message Trust, South Africa for welcoming me and giving me a platform to share my faith and work for my family.

Mark Slessenger who has mentored me.

And to everyone whom God has placed in my path, I want to thank God for using you to support me and pray for me.

Jemimah Wright is a freelance journalist and author. She is currently deputy editor of Premier's *Woman Alive* magazine. Jemimah has written five biographies, including *Never Beyond Hope* and a historical fiction novel, *Isabella's Voyage* (Instant Apostle, 2022).

A Second Chance

Breaking free from the cycle of addiction and bad choices

Simon Williams

Simon Williams' life was dominated by alcohol, illegal drugs, fraud and theft. After countless crazy escapades, including crossing a minefield on a tractor, he is caught by the authorities and put on trial in Israel.

Imprisonment does not change him, and he ends up back in prison in the UK. When his home life begins to break down, he tries to wean himself off his old habits – but can't. In despair, he shouts out to God for help and his life is changed for ever.

978-1-78893-320-9

Finding Faith in Unexpected Places

How a spiritual awakening on the hippy trail led to sharing God's love in Nepal

Geoff Walvin

A young man on the hippy trail finds more than he expected as he encounters God on his journey to find spiritual truth.

Geoff Walvin's life becomes filled with purpose as his new-found love for God leads him into difficult and dangerous places. Join Geoff on his travels and witness wonderful miracles and God's amazing provision as people living in Nepal and India are touched by the gospel and turn to Christ.

Beautifully written, uplifting and awe-inspiring, this is a story of what can happen when one person gives their life fully to Jesus Christ in total obedience and surrender.

978-1-78893-226-4

Want to dig deeper into the Bible?
Then get the full experience with the ERV Holy Bible!

Black	Floral	Teal
HB: 9781788932578	HB: 9781788932554	HB: 9781788932561

Contemporary ERV Translation - Simple to understand - Relevant and accurate.

Bursting with features to help you understand and live out God's Word today:

- Size up the setting and discover the who, when and what of each book
- Dig deeper and explore key passages with the help of 164 'Bible Bits'
- Probe passages with over 275 'Insights' that explore the meaning of verses

These Bibles are full of extra help and guides to enable you to understand what you are reading and encourage you to apply godly wisdom to your life.

Authentic

We trust you enjoyed reading this book from Authentic. If you want to be informed of any new titles from this author and other releases you can sign up to the Authentic newsletter by scanning below:

Online:
authenticmedia.co.uk

Follow us: